Oops! Word® for Windows™ What To Do When Things Go Wrong

Mike Miller
John Weingarten

que

Oops! Word for Windows

Copyright © 1993 by Que® Corporation.

Library of Congress Catalog No.: 93-84298

ISBN: 1-56529-266-9

96 95 94 93   4 3 2 1

Interpretation of the printing code: the rightmost double-digit number is the year of the book's printing; the rightmost single-digit number, the number of the book's printing. For example, a printing code of 93-1 shows that the first printing of the book occurred in 1993.

Screen reproductions in this book were created with Collage Plus from Inner Media, Inc., Hollis, NH.

This book is based on Word for Windows 2.0.

Publisher: David P. Ewing

Associate Publisher: Rick Ranucci

Operations Manager: Sheila Cunningham

Publishing Plan Manager: Thomas H. Bennett

Marketing Manager: Ray Robinson

Credits

Title Manager
Don Roche, Jr.

Acquisitions Editor
Rick Ranucci

**Product Development
Specialist**
Mike Miller

Production Editor
Heather Northrup

Editor
Elsa M. Bell

Technical Editor
Kathy Wood

Novice Reviewer
Stacey Beheler

Illustrator
John Alberti

Book Designers
Scott Cook
Amy Peppler-Adams

Production Team
Paula Carroll
Brook Farling
Carla Hall-Batton
Bob LaRoche
Jay Lesandrini
Caroline Roop
Linda Seifert
Marcella Thompson

Composed in *ITC Garamond* and *MCPdigital*
by Que Corporation

Trademarks

About the Authors

Mike Miller is the Director of Market Strategies for Prentice Hall Computer Publishing and the author of a half of a dozen computer books, including other books in the *Oops!* series and *Real Men Use DOS* for Que. Mike has been working with PCs long enough (over 10 years) to think he knows the solution to just about any problem—whether he really does or not!

John Weingarten is a computer trainer and consultant in Spokane, Washington and has written books on Lotus 1-2-3, Paradox, and WordPerfect. John has spoken computerese since the late 1970s but has taught himself English as a second language.

Contents at a Glance

Contents

3 Why Bad Things Happen to Good Word Users   39

III A Quick Course in Problem Solving

INTRODUCTION

This book is part a series of *Oops!* books from Que. Like all the other *Oops!* books, this book is written for everyday computer users like my father. He has been a computer user for more than six years, but he still runs into trouble once or twice a year. When he needs help, he turns to me. (Although, now that there's a series of *Oops!* books available, Dad's more likely to turn to an *Oops!* book than to give me a call—I guess it's easier to read the book than it is to get hold of me on the phone!) Most of my dad's computer problems, like most computer problems in general, aren't terribly serious in nature and are easily corrected—if you know what to do. This book shows you what to do.

For this book, I thought it best to collaborate with an expert, so I called on John Weingarten, who makes a living teaching users how to use Word for Windows. In this book, John and I show you how to avoid common mistakes and correct and recover from those times when you—or Word for Windows itself—do something wrong.

Who Should Read This Book?

This book is designed to be used by "normal" Word for Windows users. You don't have to be a technical expert to read this book because we don't go into a lot of technical mumbo-jumbo. John and I help you cope with common Word for Windows problems and figure out how to get things back to normal. Our comments and advice mix common sense with some tricks you might not be currently aware of. The goal is to get you up and running in the shortest possible time with the least possible fuss.

What Does This Book Discuss?

Oops! Word for Windows is divided into three major sections.

Part I, "Start Here Before Things Go Wrong," includes a lot of useful information for anyone wanting to get the most out of Word for Windows and protect himself or herself from possible problems.

Part II, "Figuring Out What Went Wrong," is the "What To Do When..." section. The individual chapters in this section get down to the core of the matter, offering specific solutions to specific problems you may encounter with Word for Windows.

Part III, "A Quick Course in Problem Solving," serves as a reference in helping you track down the causes to many common problems. I think you'll find Chapter 22, "The Great Word for Windows Trouble-shooting Road Map," to be particularly helpful in tracking down and understanding your problems.

Conventions Used in This Book

Oops! Word for Windows uses certain conventions to help you understand the text.

UPPERCASE letters are used for file names and DOS commands, such as SAMPLE.DOC and COPY.

Italic text indicates words or phrases introduced and explained for the first time, such as *cell*.

Words and keys that you press or type are indicated in a second color, such as **CD C:\DIR01**.

On-screen prompts and messages (including error messages) are indicated by a special typeface, as in General Protection Fault.

Keyboard keys are usually represented as they appear on your keyboard, such as F1 and Tab.

Key combinations are represented with the plus sign and indicate that you press and hold one key while you also press the other, as in **Alt+F**.

Finally, because I assume you'll be using Word for Windows with a mouse, I'll tell you directly which menu to pull down to access specific commands.

Plugs for Other Que Books

I don't intend for *Oops! Word for Windows* to be the only book you'll ever read about Word for Windows, so if you want a more comprehensive guide, pick up one or more of the following Que books:

- *Using Word for Windows 2,* Special Edition, a very comprehensive tutorial and reference that tells you all you'll ever want to know about Word for Windows.

- *Easy Word for Windows*, a four-color guide to basic Word for Windows procedures.

- *Word for Windows QuickStart*, an in-depth guide for beginning Word for Windows users.

- *Word for Windows Quick Reference*, a compact reference to essential Word for Windows tasks and functions.

- *Word for Windows Hot Tips*, a really good little book chock full of neat tips and tricks to help you get the most out of Word for Windows.

Finally, to troubleshoot general Windows programs, read *Oops! for Windows*, and to figure out non-Windows problems with your computer system, check out the original *Oops!* book, *Oops! What to Do When Things Go Wrong*. Tens of thousands of users have these books right beside their system units, just in case something bad happens. I recommend you do the same.

Mike Miller
April 1993

Start Here Before Things Go Wrong

ONE

Chapter 1
The 10 Most Common
Word for Windows
Problems

Chapter 2
Word for Windows Basics
for the Technically Timid

Chapter 3
Why Bad Things Happen to
Good Word for Windows
Users

Chapter 4
An Ounce of Prevention—
Preparing a Word for
Windows Survival Kit

Chapter 5
What To Do When the
Worst Happens

The 10 Most Common Word for Windows Problems

IMPORTANT: Read this chapter first!

Word for Windows can be puzzling. That's why I'm starting this book with a list of the 10 most commonly encountered problems in Word for Windows. Look over the descriptions of these problems to find the solution to your current problem (if you have one). You may put an end to your puzzlement in this first chapter.

If you solve your problem here, great! But to avoid future difficulties, read the rest of the book to learn about potential pitfalls.

Although literally thousands of potential Word for Windows problems exist, most stem from one of three causes:

- You did something wrong, such as typing a command incorrectly or accidentally hitting the wrong button.

- Your equipment is not turned on, plugged in, or connected correctly.

- Word for Windows is not installed or set up correctly.

So when you encounter a problem and feel moved to exclaim "Oops!," following these simple steps may resolve the situation:

1. Try the procedure again.

2. If the problem persists, make certain that your equipment is turned on and that all cables are connected correctly.

3. Try the procedure *one more time*.

If this doesn't alleviate the problem, take a look at the following list. Most Word for Windows users can find their solutions right here. If you don't find your problem in this list, look in the "What To Do When..." chapters for more problems and solutions.

1. You Can't Remember How To Use a Word for Windows Feature

It happens to the best of us. Word for Windows has so many features, it's tough to keep them all straight. Never fear! Help is close at hand. If you start to use a feature and get stuck, just press the Help key (F1) and Word for Windows displays a help screen for that feature. This is called *context-sensitive help*.

If you know the name of the feature you want to use, but you can't even remember how to start using the feature, choose Help Index from the Help menu and then click on the Search button. Now you can type the first letters of the feature to display a list of help features starting with those letters. Double-click on the feature you're having trouble with to see the available help topics. Click the topic you're stuck on and click the GoTo button to see a help screen for that topic.

For example, if you want to create a header, choose Help Index from the Help menu. Then click on Search and type **he**. (You only need to type the first two letters of the word headers.) Double-click on Headers: creating and editing and then, in the list of topics, double-click on Creating a header or footer. The help screen you need magically appears.

> **Tooling Around**
>
> If you're having trouble recognizing and remembering what the little icons on the toolbar are for, here's a neat way to get descriptions of each of them. Point at the mysterious button and press and hold the left mouse button. The status bar displays a description of the button's function.
>
> If you release the mouse button while the mouse pointer is still pointing at the toolbar button, you activate the feature. If you don't want to use the feature, drag the mouse pointer into the work area and release the mouse button.

You can also find extensive help in other Word for Windows books from Que, such as *Using Word for Windows 2,* Special Edition. If you don't know the name of the feature you need, read on.

2. You Accidentally Deleted Some Text

You press the Delete key and then realize you need that block of text after all. No problem. Word for Windows can undo just about any mistake you make.

To undo the deletion you just made, pull down the Edit menu and choose Undo Edit Clear. To undo a formatting change you just made, choose Undo Formatting from the Edit menu. The Undo command reflects the last action you took; the text you erased reappears.

Saving your work on a regular basis can save you from all sorts of deletion trauma. If you save your work before making any major editing changes, you can simply close the file without saving it and open the original again if you make a major mess.

3. You Accidentally Typed Some Text in ALL CAPS

You must have hit the Caps Lock key by mistake. Don't worry, you don't need to retype anything. Converting text from uppercase to lowercase is a snap. If you just need to convert a single word, make sure the insertion point is in that word and press **Shift+F3**. The first letter of the word remains in uppercase. If you want *all* the letters in lowercase, press **Shift+F3** again.

If you need to convert several words or sentences, select the text you want to convert and use **Shift+F3** until the text is the way you want it. You may have to do a bit of editing after a case conversion, perhaps capitalizing the first letter of each sentence, but that's sure better than retyping the whole thing.

4. You Can't Find Your Document

This is the worst. You spent hours (days?) creating an important document and you can't remember where it is and/or what you named it.

When Word for Windows is installed on your computer, it normally specifies a *working directory* called C:\WINWORD in which files are saved and opened. The problem with this scheme is that this directory is where all the Word for Windows program files are located. You can end up with some big-time clutter if you also store your document files here.

To keep your documents separate from Word for Windows program files, make a directory on your hard disk for your documents and tell Word for Windows to use it as the default directory. You can create a new directory from Windows' File Manager or from the DOS prompt. Give your new directory a name such as

> ### Get Down with DOS
>
> If you want to know more of the nitty-gritty details about DOS directories and how files are organized on your hard disk, check out one of the many terrific Que books devoted to interpreting DOS technobabble, such as *I Hate DOS* or *MS-DOS 6 QuickStart*.

C:\WINWORD\MYFILES. If you don't know how to create a new directory on your hard disk, take a look at Chapter 8, "What To Do When...Your File Is Missing."

The easiest way to make this directory the default directory is to modify the properties for the Word for Windows icon in Windows' Program Manager.

Switch to the Program Manager by pressing **Ctrl+Esc** to display the Task List and double-clicking on Program Manager. Next, click once on the Microsoft Word icon. Pull down the **F**ile menu and choose **P**roperties. Tab to the Working Directory box, and enter the name of your new directory, **C:\WINWORD\MYFILES** for example, and press **Enter** to accept the changes. Word for Windows doesn't use the new working directory setting until you exit and restart the program.

Okay, that takes care of missing files for the future. But what about the file whose name you can't remember? Do a search for all the files in a directory that contain a specific word or phrase. Choose **O**pen from the **F**ile menu to display the Open dialog box. Click on the Find File button to open the Find File dialog box. Next, click on the Search button to show the Search dialog box.

The File Name text box probably contains `*.DOC`, which means that when you start the search, Word for Windows only finds files with a DOC extension. If all your Word for Windows documents have a DOC extension, this setting is fine. If you want to search for files with any extension, however, replace the `*.DOC` with *.*.

Enter a word or phrase you know your document contains in the Any Text text box and press **Enter** to start the search. You end up with a list of files that contain the word or phrase. See? Word for Windows doesn't let you lose a file.

If Word for Windows doesn't find the file you're looking for, you may have to repeat the Find procedure in several directories. You can change the directory that Word for Windows searches in the Location section of the Search dialog box. You can also have Word for Windows search your entire hard disk drive by opening the Search dialog box, choosing the drive to search, choosing Edit Path, and then choosing Delete All. This procedure can take a while, so save it as a last resort.

5. Your Lines of Text Don't Adjust When You Insert or Delete Words

Many Happy Returns

You can easily remove the extra carriage returns (caused by pressing **Enter** at the end of each line) by using the Replace feature. Pull down the **Edit** menu and choose Replace. Type ^p in the Find What text box. Don't put anything in the Replace With text box and then choose Replace All. Voila! No more extra returns!

You've been pressing **Enter** at the end of each line, haven't you? This habit is common among people who are accustomed to working on a typewriter.

If you press **Enter** at the end of each line of text, Word for Windows can't reformat the lines as you edit them. Let the program adjust the text for you with its *word wrap* feature. Not only will this feature make future editing easier, but, once you get used to it, it will save you typing time.

6. Your Headers, Footers, and Page Numbers Don't Display On-Screen

Word for Windows only displays headers, footers, and page numbers (and several other features) in Page Layout view and Print Preview. You can choose Page Layout view for a more accurate approximation of what your printed pages will look like by choosing **Page Layout** from the **View** menu.

Of course, there's a catch. Page Layout view is slower than Normal or Draft, especially if your document contains graphic objects. Furthermore, there are some things Word for Windows doesn't show you even in Page Layout view, such as line numbers and graphic lines between columns.

> ### Change Your View
>
> If you want to zip out to Page Layout view from Print Preview, simply double-click on the Print Preview window.

You can only see these elements when you print or go into Print Preview by choosing Print Preview from the **File** menu.

7. Font Changes and Other Character Attributes Don't Display

If you're in Draft view, all the text in your document looks the same. Text that has some attribute applied to it is underlined. To see the different fonts, bold, italic, and so on, switch to Normal or Page Layout view by choosing **Normal** or **Page Layout** from the **View** menu.

> ### Don't Dodge the Draft!
>
> There is an advantage to working in Draft view—it takes less time to do things to your document, especially if your document contains a lot of graphics.

8. Columns of Text or Numbers Aren't Aligned Properly When You Print, But They Look OK On-Screen

This problem is caused by using the space bar to line up columns of text and numbers (a big no-no). If you print with proportional fonts (most people do) and use the space bar to line up columns, your columns snake down the page like this:

Joe	123.00	12/28/93
Mary	1029.33	12/29/93
Fred	47.99	1/11/94
Sally	107.23	2/18/94

The cure is simple—use tabs instead of spaces to create these *tabular columns*. Set one tab stop for each column. Moving to a tab stop takes your insertion point to a specific position, which is the same every time regardless of the preceding text. See Chapter 13 for more information.

Another approach to consider for columns is the Table feature. This feature organizes rows and columns into rectangular boxes called cells, which makes for easier formatting. See Chapter 16 for more table talk.

9. You Encounter the Dreaded Font Change Nightmare

Your document contains a number of sections and each has a heading with type that's about 50% larger than the body text. You selected and changed each heading to larger type.

Here's the nightmare part. You decide the body text should be a little smaller so your document fits on fewer pages. Of course, you also want each of the headings to be proportionately smaller. Uh oh! There's no easy way to do it. You'd have to change the font before and after every heading. If only you'd used Word for Windows' Style feature.

By applying styles with the appropriate characteristics to your headings and text

> **Fontasizing**
>
> If you're just moving to computers from typewriters or don't have a printer that prints proportional fonts, you may be used to terms like pitch or CPI (Characters Per Inch). That's how fixed-width fonts are measured. Because each character in a proportionally spaced font occupies a different amount of horizontal space, CPI is no longer relevant. That's why proportional fonts are specified in *points*, which measure the height of the characters. (One point is roughly 1/72 of an inch high. Typical body text is 10 to 12 points.)

paragraphs, you can change the characteristics of the entire document by simply redefining the styles.

Word for Windows comes with several pre-defined styles, but you can easily add your own custom styles. The easiest way to define a new style is to format a paragraph with all the characteristics you want in your style. Then select the paragraph and double-click on the style name on the ribbon and enter a new name for your style (up to 24 characters). When you click in the work area, the new style is defined and can be applied to other portions of the document. See Chapter 18 for more style information.

10. Your Printer Doesn't Print

The most common printer problems are also the simplest to solve. If your printer refuses to print, make certain first that it is plugged in. Then check to ensure that the printer is turned on and that it is on-line. (This is usually indicated by some light on the front of the printer.) Next, confirm that your printer has plenty of paper and that none of it is jammed in the mechanism. If you've just run out of paper and added more, you may need to turn your printer off and back on again to reset the printing process. Finally, make sure that the printer cable is plugged firmly into both your printer and your system unit.

If after all these checks your printer *still* doesn't work, make sure the printer is properly set up and selected in Word for Windows. Pull down the File menu and choose Print Setup. The Print Setup dialog box tells you what the currently selected printer is and allows you to change the selection and modify its options.

Other Problems

If this chapter doesn't address your specific problem, don't panic! The book contains 21 additional chapters, one of which may hold the key. If you can isolate the general cause of your problem (printing, columns, etc.), turn to the chapter that addresses that topic. If you can't determine even the general problem area, go directly to Chapter 22, "The Great Troubleshooting Road Map," to track down the likely culprit.

Don't worry if some of the information presented in this chapter seems foreign to you. Just turn the page and proceed to Chapter 2, a refresher course on the Word for Windows basics you need to get (and keep) yourself out of trouble.

Word Basics for the Technically Timid

Before you begin editing macros, merging data, and building tables, you may find it useful to take a quick refresher course in Word for Windows basics. The best way to start is by examining the various parts of the Windows environment—what they do and what problems they can cause.

Now, don't let all this initial attention to Windows details disturb you. This book is written for you, the average computer user, not some techno-dweeb who carries a screwdriver set in a pocket protector. I'm only going to tell you about what's vital to understand about Windows as it applies to Word for Windows. If you're looking for super-technical details about the difference between WIN.INI and SYSTEM.INI files, forget it—this isn't the place to find that sort of technospeak. But if you want to learn about how to avoid the pitfalls *real people* encounter with Windows and Word for Windows, this is the chapter for you!

All About Windows

I assume you have your hardware (the computer and printer) set up, plugged in, and turned on, with all the cables connected properly. If this is not true, please make it so. Now let's explore Word and Windows.

Opening New Windows

Windows is, technically, an operating environment. It employs a *graphical user interface* (abbreviated GUI and sometimes pronounced gooey) to shield you from the often bewildering world of DOS. Windows uses pull-down menus and a whole bunch of *icons* to pictorially represent programs and operations on-screen. Windows can also perform multiple operations simultaneously. This *multitasking* capability enables Windows to run more than one program at a time.

To perform most operations in Windows, all you need to do is use the mouse to pull down a menu or click an icon to perform most operations.

The Mighty Mouse

To use Windows with a mouse, you need to learn a few simple mouse operations. When you *click* (press and release) a *mouse button*, you initiate an action. *Dragging* is moving the mouse while holding down the mouse button. You usually use this technique to move an object from one part of the screen to another or to *select* (highlight) text so that it can be manipulated. *Double-clicking* (pressing the mouse button twice in quick succession) is frequently used as a shortcut to executing a procedure.

The main Windows interface (what you see) is called the *Program Manager*. The Program Manager can hold many separate *program groups*, which are analogous to file folders (and appear as such on-screen). Each program group, when opened, contains a number of individual programs. The Main and Accessories program groups, for example, contain all the main Windows mini-applications such as File Manager, Print Manager, and Paintbrush.

To open a program group, point to it with your mouse pointer and double-click the main (usually left) mouse button. The group expands on-screen from an icon to a *window* (a mini-screen within the screen) to display its contents.

Identifying Files

Your computer system uses *files* to store data; all electronically generated data is, in fact, organized into files. Files can consist of documents created by Word for Windows, listings of fields created by your database, or even the core codes of your application programs themselves. To operate your computer at all, you must know how to work with its files.

Every file on your computer has its own unique name. You must follow certain conventions for naming files in order for DOS to understand exactly which file you want when you try to access one. Each file's name consists of three parts, as described in the following table.

Name	The first part of the file name consists of up to 8 characters, which can include either letters or numbers.
Period	Sometimes referred to as "dot," the period following the name acts as a divider between the name and the extension.
Extension	This last part of the name consists of up to 3 characters, including either letters or numbers, and is used to denote various types of files. The period and extension often are optional when naming a file.

Putting all these parts together, you get file names that appear on-screen something like `FILENAME.EXT`.

And just what can you do with your files? File Manager and Word for Windows' Find File feature let you do all sorts of things to your files. You can copy files from one place to another, delete files you no longer need, rename files, see a listing of files on your disk, and even view the contents of certain types of files before deciding what to do with them.

How Word and Windows Are Linked

You only get the real benefits of Windows if you use it with a Windows application such as Word for Windows. Word for Windows takes advantage of all the standard Windows features, and, perhaps because it was written by Microsoft (the company that wrote Windows), Word is even better integrated in some ways with its Windows environment than many other Windows applications.

Word for Windows (like other Windows applications) relies on Windows to handle most of the computer's interaction with the screen and printer, freeing Word for Windows to concentrate on what it does best—word processing.

If Word for Windows is your only Windows application, you don't realize the full benefit of the environment. As you add programs, if you have a choice between a Windows version and a DOS version, you're almost always better off choosing the Windows version.

All About Word for Windows

You're using a state-of-the-art word processing program that has more features and methods for using those features than you can shake a mouse at. Before jumping into solving the myriad problems you may encounter, I'm presenting a brief refresher course on word processing in general and Word for Windows in particular.

Word Processing 101

The beauty of word processing is that you never have to retype anything. Back in the Stone Age (the typewriter era), getting words onto paper was a real drag. You had to type very carefully so as not to make any mistakes. When you made mistakes, you had to get out the correction tape, apply correction fluid, or (oh no!) retype your document.

A word processor can actually improve the quality of your writing by allowing you to fine-tune your work before committing it to paper. You can edit, move, or delete paragraphs easily. You can bring in text from another word processing document or even another type of program, such as a spreadsheet or graphics application. And, before you print, you can use my favorite part of a modern word processing program, the spell checker, to catch most of those nasty typos and spelling errors.

Another basic feature that all word processing programs have in common is *word wrap*. Word wrap lets you type continuously without having to press the **Enter** key at the end of each line. In fact, you shouldn't press the **Enter** key except when ending a paragraph or typing short lines, such as a date or address. It's word wrap that lets your word processor reformat the text when changes are made. You can change margins, line spacing, tab stops, and fonts, and the text ends up where it should.

Why Is Word for Windows Special?

Word for Windows is the result of many years of improvements in word processing programs. Word for Windows shows you, onscreen, an amazingly accurate approximation of what you'll see on the printed page. In addition, Word for Windows puts at your command the tools to accomplish every conceivable document preparation task. You can go far beyond conventional word processing with merging (for mass mailings), macros (to automate word processing tasks), tables, graphs, drawings, pictures, collapsible outlines, grammar checking, and so many more features it would take several books to completely explain them all.

So, what's so special about Word for Windows? It does it all. And, after you learn the ins and outs of the program, you'll find that it does it all with ease.

What Word for Windows *Can't* Do

As incredibly advanced as Word is, you still need to think while creating your documents. For example, Word can't correct your spelling errors by itself. All its spell checker can do is stop at words that don't appear in its built-in dictionary and ask how you want to resolve the problem.

When doing a mail merge, you still need to set up your data files so they contain the information required for the documents they will be merged with. Word won't decide for you what margins or fonts you should use.

Remember that Word can only do what you tell it to do. And it may not always be able to warn you if you're telling it to do something stupid or tell you how to correct a mistake you made. That's where this book comes in.

Getting Around

What you see when you first start Word for Windows is a mostly blank screen with some funny little squares with pictures on them, a bunch of arrows and some words that look like they might have something to do with word processing. Let's take a tour of the opening screen.

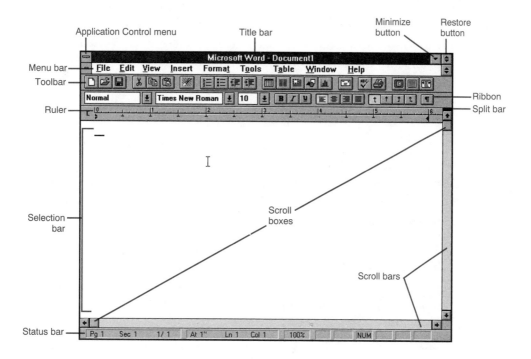

Clicking on the program's or a document's *Application Control menu* gives you a quick way to control that window. For example, you can close a document or program by double-clicking on its Application Control menu.

The *title bar* tells you the name of the program you're using (in case you forgot) and the name of the document that's currently on-screen. When you first start Word, there isn't any document on-screen, so Word calls your first, nameless document Document1 (pretty creative, eh?).

The *menu bar* lists the headings for all the pull-down menus. Clicking on one of the menu headings causes Windows to display the full menu. Some of the options in pull-down menus are followed by an ellipsis (...), which indicates that a *dialog box* full of other options appears when you choose that menu option.

The *minimize* and *maximize* buttons let you control the size of a window. Clicking the minimize button reduces Word for Windows to an icon. Clicking the *maximize* button enlarges the program or document to its largest size on-screen. When you click the maximize button, you'll have a minimize and a *restore* button. The restore button reduces the size of the window to its pre-maximized size.

The *toolbar* buttons provide shortcuts for many of the commonly used features in Word for Windows. Just click on a button to access that feature. You can even customize the toolbar to gain quick access to your favorite features. See Chapter 17 for information on customizing toolbars.

The *ribbon* lets you format your paragraphs and characters without having to wade through layers of menus. You can change style and font, bold, underline, or italicize characters, change the alignment of paragraphs, add tab stops, and display or hide nonprinting characters.

The *ruler* gives you a reference point for your text and displays margin markers and any custom tab stops.

The *split bar* lets you divide the current document window into two horizontal *panes*. You can view different portions of the document in each pane and scroll them independently.

The *scroll bars* let you quickly move through your document by clicking the arrows at the ends of the scroll bars or dragging the *scroll boxes* within the scroll bars.

The *selection bar* is an invisible vertical strip along the left side of the document. By positioning the mouse pointer in this area you can select large chunks of text. You can tell when the mouse pointer is in the selection bar because it turns into a diagonal arrow with the tip pointing toward about two o'clock.

The *status bar*, located at the bottom of the screen, gives you some useful information about your current document. At the far left, you see your current page number. Next, you find the section number (you can have Word break documents into sections) and page x of y (where x is the current page and y is the total number of pages in the document). Moving to the right you see the insertion point's distance from the top edge of the page and how many lines (regardless of type size) the insertion point is from the top of the document. Col refers to the number of characters your insertion point is from the left edge of the document. The percentage figure displays the amount of enlargement or reduction of your document's view.

The status bar also displays a number of other conditions, such as OVR (overtype mode), CAPS (Caps Lock), and NUM (Num Lock). The status bar also displays messages describing commands or the progress of some operations. For example, if you point to a toolbar button and hold down the left mouse button, the status bar displays that button's function.

Getting Words On-Screen

When you first start Word, if you haven't made any changes to the defaults, a *document window* appears on-screen, just waiting to receive your text, so just start typing.

Remember: only press the Enter key to end paragraphs and short lines such as dates and addresses.

When you need to correct a typo, position the insertion point where you need to make the correction and press the Delete key

Line 'em Up

When you press the Enter key, Word treats the preceding text (up to the last place the Enter key was pressed) as a paragraph. If you type an address like this

Jane Smith
123 Pine Street
Spokane, WA 99201

and end each line by pressing Enter, you have three paragraphs on your hands. The problem is, if you want to format all three paragraphs the same way, you have to make sure you select all three paragraphs before formatting.

If you want Word to treat the lines of an address as a table instead three separate paragraphs, insert a *new line symbol* after each line by pressing Shift+Enter.

to erase the character to the right of the insertion point or press the Backspace key to erase the character to the left. When you need to erase more than a few characters, select the unwanted text and press the **Delete** or **Backspace** key.

If you accidentally delete some text, immediately choose Edit, Undo Edit Clear to restore the text. Make sure it's the very next thing you do because Word can only undo the very last thing you've done.

Selecting Text

Before you can apply character formatting attributes to your existing text, you need a way to tell Word which text you want the attribute applied to. The process of indicating which text you want manipulated is called *selecting*. Selected text appears highlighted on-screen. You can select text by dragging the mouse over it. Remember, dragging just means moving the mouse while holding down the left mouse button. You can drag horizontally to select text a character at a time or drag vertically to select a line at a time.

There are also a few selection shortcuts. To select a word, position the I-beam pointer anywhere on the word and double-click. You can select the entire line by moving the mouse pointer into the selection bar and clicking next to the line you want to select. Double-clicking in the selection bar next to a paragraph selects the entire paragraph. If you want to select multiple paragraphs, you can double-click and hold the left mouse button and drag up or down. The entire document can be selected by holding down the **Ctrl** key while clicking in the selection bar.

Getting It Write

Word for Windows is, to use a little literary license, an object-oriented word processor. When you edit or format your document, you are working on an object at one of three levels: character, paragraph, or section.

Character Formatting

Formatting characters is simply a matter of turning on some character attributes and typing some text. If the characters are already typed, you can select the characters (from one character to the entire document) and then turn on the attributes. For example, to bold a word that has already been typed, select the word and click on the B button on the ribbon.

If you want to apply multiple character attributes simultaneously, pull down the Format menu and choose the Character option. In the Character dialog box, click in as many of the style check boxes as you like, change the font or point size of the type, and specify any other formatting changes you want to apply before clicking OK to close the dialog box. If you want your changes to become default character format settings, click on the Use as Default button before closing the dialog box.

When you turn on a character formatting attribute before typing any text, the attribute stays in effect until you change it. For example, if you turn on the italics attribute, all the text you type from that point on will be italicized until you turn off the italics attribute.

Paragraph Formatting

The paragraph is the heart of Word for Windows. When you press the **Enter** key, Word inserts a nonprinting *paragraph symbol* (¶), which tells Word you created a new paragraph. Even if you press the **Enter** key a couple of times to create a couple of blank lines, Word inserts paragraph symbols and considers each line a paragraph.

That paragraph symbol is important. Word stores all the formatting for a paragraph in the paragraph symbol that ends the paragraph. It's also important to understand that paragraphs acquire their formatting from the preceding paragraph. If the last paragraph is left-aligned with tab stops every 1 1/2 inches and double-spaced, the next paragraph has all the same properties.

You can change the paragraph formatting for any paragraph by just positioning the insertion point anywhere in the paragraph and choosing the formatting attributes you want. The changes don't affect other existing paragraphs, but the changes *will* affect any new paragraphs you type directly after the paragraph you change.

When Word for Windows is installed, the paragraph symbols are invisible. You can make them visible by clicking on the ¶ button on the ribbon. Clicking on the ¶ button again toggles them back off. Word also employs nonprinting characters to represent spaces, tabs, optional hyphens, and hidden text. You can control which (if any) of these are visible when the ¶ button is toggled to display nonprinting characters.

To designate which nonprinting characters to display, choose Options from the Tools pull-down menu and make sure the View category is highlighted. Click in the check boxes next to the nonprinting characters you want to display. If you want them all displayed, click in the check box next to All.

Because deleting a paragraph symbol causes the current paragraph to take on the formatting attributes of the previous paragraph and can wreak havoc with your document, it's crucial to know where they are so you don't accidentally demolish one. I can't stress strongly enough that you should do all your work in Word with the paragraph symbols visible.

Word's philosophy of paragraphs makes more sense as you familiarize yourself with the program. The best way to understand the concept is to make some of the mistakes detailed throughout the book and then dig yourself out.

Section Formatting

Sections give you the ability to format different portions of a document with completely different properties. For example, you can have a section with 1/2" margins and three columns set up to print on 8 1/2" by 14" paper in *landscape* (sideways) orientation, and have another section set up for 1" margins in a single column with 8 1/2" by 11" paper in *portrait* (normal) orientation. Sections are invaluable in long or complex (or both) documents.

Anytime you want to insert a new section, pull down the Insert menu and choose Break. Click on one of the Section Break buttons.

- The Next Page button starts the new section at the top of the next page.

- Continuous inserts a section break right where your insertion point is on the current page. This option is great if you want to change margin or column formatting for just a portion of the page.

- The Even Page button inserts a section break and starts a new page, and forces the new page to be an even-numbered page. This option ensures that the page is on the left when printing a document that will be double-sided.

- The Odd Page option is just like the Even Page option, but it forces the new section to start on an odd (right-hand) page.

How Do You Spell Relief?

After you type your document, you should make sure the spelling is purfect, I mean, perfect. Word's spell checker is just the ticket for catching most spelling errors and typos.

To start the spell checker, choose Spelling from the Tools menu and the spell checker immediately starts scanning the document for words that don't match any word in its dictionary, as well as repeated words and words with irregular capitalization. When the spell checker catches a suspected problem, it highlights the suspect word and displays a dialog box with several options. You can also click the ABC button to start the spell checker.

The first piece of information in the dialog box lets you know what sort of problem Word thinks it has encountered. If a word in the

document doesn't match a word in the dictionary, the message is
Not in Dictionary. Word usually has some suggestions for alternative words, and the one it thinks is the most likely candidate appears in the Change To text box. If the word in the Change To text box is the word you really meant to type, click on the Change button, or, if you want Word to change any other occurrences of the misspelled word in the document, click on Change All.

If the word in the Change To text box isn't correct, click on the correct word in the Suggestions list. When you click on a suggested word, that word appears in the Change To text box. If none of the suggestions are correct, you can edit the word yourself in the Change To text box and then click on Change. If you still don't have it right, Word asks you whether you really want to continue this operation with a word that isn't in the dictionary. If you respond by clicking on the Yes button, Word dutifully obeys. If you say no, Word display the Spelling dialog box again with suggestions for the new word. Pick one of the new suggestions, do some additional editing, or call a friendly English professor.

Sometimes a word in the document is so weird that Word doesn't have a clue as to what you mean. In that event, the Suggestions list says something really helpful: No Suggestions. If the word as you originally typed it is the way you want it, click on Ignore or Ignore All to leave any other occurrences of the word.

Lots of words you use in your line of work (whatever it is), such as product names, people's names, and so on, aren't in the dictionary. If you don't want to have to tell Word what to do with each of these more than once, add them to the dictionary.

When you add words to the dictionary, you're not adding them to the main dictionary that came with Word; you're adding them to a custom dictionary that is created as you

---

Editing the Custom Dictionary

You may have a long list of words you want to add to the custom dictionary. Or you may want to delete or correct some words you added to it earlier. No problem. Just open CUSTOM.DIC in the WINWORD directory. This is a *text file* and Word asks whether you want to convert it. You need to click on OK so Word can open the file. When you're done editing, use the Save As command on the File menu to save the file as Text Only.

add words to it. To add a word to the custom dictionary, click on the Add button.

Follow the same basic guidelines for repeated words or irregularly capitalized words and you'll do just fine. If your insertion point wasn't at the beginning of the document when you started the spell-check process, Word checks from that point forward and then asks whether you want to continue checking at the beginning of the document. Click on Yes to have Word inspect the portion of the document you may have missed.

If you realize you made a mistake when you told Word how to re-solve a problem, click the Undo Last button and Word undoes the last speller action, even if it was adding a word to the custom dictionary.

Saving Your Work

One of the most important Word for Windows skills is knowing how to save your documents. You need to save your work-in-progress to disk often enough that, if the electricity goes out just before the next time you're about to save, you won't be too upset at losing that amount of work. For most people, somewhere between 10 and 20 minutes is a reasonable amount of work to lose. I hate to sound so negative, but this is something I want you to be scared about.

The easiest way to save your work is to click on the Save toolbar but-ton (the one that has a picture of a 3 1/2" disk on it). The first time you save a document, Word displays the Save As dialog box. All you need to do at this point is type a name for your document. You have up to eight characters. You can even add a three-letter extension after the period, but Word adds a DOC extension if you don't specify one of your own.

When the document has a name, you can click the Save button and then just go on typing. Word saves the new version of your docu-ment, replacing the older version. There is more discussion about saving files in Chapter 3. Stay tuned.

Opening a File

To open (retrieve) a file from your computer's disk, click on the Open toolbar button (the one that has a picture of an open file folder on it). The Open dialog box appears, prompting you to tell Word which file you want opened.

The File Name text box contains a pattern so Word knows which files to list. The pattern is usually *.doc which tells Word to display a list of files starting with any file name and ending with the extension .doc. If the file you're looking for is in the File Name list, double-click on it, and it appears on-screen. If the file you want isn't on the list, check the Directories and Drives section of the dialog box. If the drive is correct but the directory isn't, double-click on the correct directory or move up a level on the directory tree and proceed down another branch.

If the file you're looking for ends with something other than .DOC, select DOC in the File Name text box and type the extension you want. If you want to look for files ending with *any* extension, enter * (asterisk) in place of DOC.

If the current directory is C:\WINDOWS but the file you want is in the C:\WINWORD directory, you have to move up a level to the C:\ directory and then back down to the C:\WINWORD directory. To accomplish this, double-click on C:\ in the directories list and then double-click on WINWORD in the list. You may need to scroll down in the list until WINWORD is visible.

All That's Fit To Print

The final step in creating your document is printing. If you want to print your entire document, nothing could be easier. First, make sure the printer is properly connected to the computer and is turned on and toggled to the on-line mode, with paper loaded. Now, click on the Print toolbar button. That's it! Your entire document is sent to the printer without any further fuss or muss.

If you want to modify some of the print options, such as printing specific pages or multiple copies of the document, choose Print from the File menu to display the Print dialog box. From there, you can direct Word to print your document the way you want it printed. You can even choose which printer to print on, if you have more than one printer.

If the printed pages don't look the way they should, check out Chapter 11, "What To Do When...Your Printer Doesn't Print Right."

Wrapping It Up

This chapter is intended as a crash course in what Windows and Word for Windows can do and how to do it. If you want to know more, check out Que's *Using Word for Windows 2,* Special Edition. Books like this one contain lots of comprehensive information on the program, and are good references for any level of user.

Now, turn the page and learn something really important—why bad things happen to good computer users!

Why Bad Things Happen to Good Word Users

You're a good person. (I know you must be—after all, you bought this book, didn't you?) So why should you be the victim of Word for Windows problems? Don't you deserve better than this?

Of course you do! But the reality is that Word problems can befall anyone. And no matter how careful you are, the chances are good that at some time in your computing career something will go wrong. Your mission, therefore (should you decide to accept it), is to ensure that nothing major goes wrong and that you're as thoroughly prepared as possible for whatever does happen, however minor.

The Source of the Problem

Most problems are easy to solve, because they're really not major problems. Oh, they may appear to be major, but in reality, they are easily fixed. Let's take a look at some of the most common sources of Word problems and how you can avoid them.

Most of the problems discussed in this section are not specific to Word, but apply equally to your work with any computer program. You've learned enough about your computer system and Word for Windows in Chapters 1 and 2 that you're now ready to face these problems head-on. So have at it.

Garbage In, Garbage Out

The most common cause of Word problems is, bar none, *you*! Now, don't take offense at this, but most problems result when the user (yes, that's you!) does something wrong. You may not *know* you're doing something wrong, but you do it anyway.

When you make an error at your computer, you almost always do so accidentally, and you usually remain unaware of your blunder—at least until

What's All This Fuss About Garbage?

The phrase *garbage in, garbage out* refers to a phenomenon not particularly unique to computers. When you input garbage (you make a mistake), the computer is too stupid (actually too *literal*) to interpret what you meant to do and outputs exactly what you input. So, if you put garbage in, you get garbage out. After all, computers can't read your mind...yet.

something goes terribly and unmistakably wrong with your work. The key to correcting the problem, however, is to remain calm and retrace your steps to figure out exactly what you did wrong.

Read the following sections closely. They describe the two most common user errors. One of these mistakes may very well be the root of your own problem.

Bad Typing

The most common errors inevitably occur when you type something wrong. If you're like me, your fingers occasionally fly across the keyboard faster than you're actually able to type, and they usually do so when you're looking at anything but the screen. You may want to try typing a little more slowly in the future. (Remember the tortoise and the hare.) If you find that you have trouble typing accurately even at slower speeds, consider taking a typing course or buying a typing instruction program for your computer. You'd be surprised how much these things can increase both your typing speed and your accuracy.

Are You the Right Type?

You can actually use your computer to help you type better on your computer. Several typing instruction software programs can help you improve the speed and accuracy of your typing (or *keyboarding*, as computer nerds might refer to it). The program I recommend is (surprise!) *Typing Tutor* from Que Software. Ask for it by name wherever you shop for software.

Those Pesky Plugs!

After you eliminate typing errors as the source of your problems, check for the second most common cause of computer malfunctions: improper hookup. Hooking up a handful of cables may sound simple, but it's easy to do wrong. If you plug a cable into the wrong connector, whatever is connected to that cable won't work. If the connection isn't solid (the plug is loose), operation can be intermittent. If the cable is old or frayed, or sharply bent, the wires inside the cable may not transmit data effectively, again causing intermittent operation. And, of course, if you forget to turn the power on, nothing happens at all!

It's a Setup!

You must configure Word for Windows to work with the equipment in your system. Many problems result when users fail to set up their software correctly. For example, if a LaserJet printer is hooked up to your system, but Word is set up to use a dot-matrix printer, your printed output is going to look messed up.

Changes Beget Changes

If you change any aspect of your system—for example, if you upgrade to a better monitor or add a new printer—you must change Windows' settings to reflect your new hardware. If you don't, Windows doesn't know you've changed something, and keeps on acting the same old way, which may not be the right way to work with your new equipment.

To let Windows know about display, keyboard, mouse, or network changes, open Windows Setup from the Main program group in Program Manager. The Windows Setup dialog box lists your currently specified equipment. Choose Change System Settings from the Options menu and make the needed changes. If you change printers or add fonts, make these modifications through the Fonts and Printers dialog boxes, which are accessible through the Control Panel in the Main Program group.

Fortunately, Windows and Word for Windows (and most software programs) configure themselves when you first install them on your system. But occasionally, an installation program doesn't work quite right, and you may experience really strange operational problems. If you are having these sorts of problems, check your software settings.

If, for any reason, you discover your settings are incorrect, *change them*! Most programs enable you to edit their settings after installation, either by using menu options or a separate setup program.

What Can Go Wrong with Word for Windows

Part Two of this book focuses on specific Word for Windows problems and how to avoid them, but here are some of the more common ones you are likely to run into.

Choosing the Wrong Command

When choosing menu commands from the keyboard, you must use the underlined letter. It's an easy mistake to pick the first letter of the menu name, which often isn't the correct letter to invoke that menu. For example, **Alt+F** opens the File menu, but **Alt+T** opens the Format menu. If you choose the wrong menu, you can usually back out of it by pressing the **Esc** key.

Choosing a toolbar button by mistake is also an easy trap. Perhaps you click on the printer button on the toolbar and, before your finger has even released the mouse button, you know you messed up. Next time this happens with a toolbar button, keep that finger on the mouse button! Until you release the mouse button, the command isn't executed. With your finger still holding down the mouse button, drag the mouse pointer down into the document area and then release the mouse button. Word for Windows ignores the toolbar command.

The Disappearing Word

It can certainly be a shock when, with one click of the mouse, Word for Windows vanishes without a trace. The most common way to lose Word is to click on the minimize button. This action reduces Word to an icon which is often hidden behind other windows or applications. If the Microsoft Word icon is visible, simply double-click on it to restore the program to its former size.

If the icon isn't visible, the easiest way to get Word going again is with the Task List. Press **Ctrl+Esc** to invoke the Task List dialog box, which lists all currently running programs. Click on Microsoft Word in the list and then click on the Switch To button.

WYSIWYG Won't

You bought Word for Windows so that your fonts and graphics appear on-screen the way they will print. If they don't, one likely cause is that you accidentally chose Draft mode from the View pull-down menu. Fonts and graphics only appear properly when Draft isn't selected. To turn off Draft mode, choose Draft from the View menu again.

You Can't Remember How To Start a New Document

You've finished with the document on-screen, and you're ready to start a new one. There are so many options that figuring out which is the correct one can be a bit intimidating. Choose New from the File pull-down menu and then choose OK to start a new document based on the Normal template. To base your new document on a different template, highlight the template in the Use Template list and then choose OK. A shortcut for starting a new document based on the Normal template is to click on the New Document button on the toolbar. Word for Windows gives you a clean slate on which to create your new masterpiece.

Your Screen Is Missing Some Important Pieces

The toolbar, ribbon, and ruler make so many tasks easier, it's hard to imagine how you'd get along without them. If, one day, one or all of these terrific aids is missing, chances are you accidentally clicked on the tool name in the View menu. For example, if the ruler is not there, choose Ruler from the View menu. There may be times when you'll actually *want* to rid your screen of one or more of these tools to gain more real estate for your document. That's fine, as long as that's what you intended to do.

Your Fonts Are Getting Larger When They Should Be Getting Smaller

You know from your typewriter experience that when you choose type with a larger number, the type gets smaller. That's because the numbers for the type on typewriters (and older computers) meant characters per inch. The larger the number, the more characters would fit in an inch. In Word for Windows, however, when you choose larger numbers, the type gets larger.

What gives? In Word for Windows the numbers generally refer to points, which measure the height of the type. There are approximately 72 points to an inch. With point sizes, the larger the number, the larger the type. So, Word *is* working correctly. You just need to adjust your thinking.

How To Be a Better Word User

How can you become an even better computer user than you already are? The next few sections provide you with some helpful suggestions.

Be Careful

You should always take extra care to prevent making mistakes whenever you use Word. If you type a command, be sure to type it correctly. (It helps if you actually *look at the screen* while you're typing, especially before you press the **Enter** key to execute a command!) If you're pushing a button or choosing a menu item, make sure you're doing the right thing before you click that mouse button. But remember, you can always use the Undo command.

Follow Proper Procedures

If you follow a few basic, common-sense procedures, you'll save yourself quite a bit of time and frustration, and possibly prevent loss of your valuable data.

The first procedure to remember is to save your work frequently. This theme is repeated often in this book because this is the most important procedure to remember. The next section on making copies discusses saving, but something you might want to consider *in addition* to saving your work manually is enabling Word's automatic save feature if it has accidentally been turned off.

To turn it on, choose Options from the Tools menu to open the Options dialog box. Use the up or down arrow keys to highlight the Save category and then make sure the check box in front of Automatic Save Every is checked. Finally, use the up or down arrow next to the text box to change the number of minutes between saves. Usually somewhere between 10 and 20 minutes is about right.

When you finish creating a document, and sometimes before you finish, the next step is to print it. Hold on just a minute. You can save paper and time if you get in the habit of using Print Preview before you print your work. As good as Word is at showing you what your document will look like prior to printing, the Normal and Page Layout views don't give you a 100% accurate picture.

If you print your document and then realize it requires formatting changes, you've wasted the paper to do the first printing and the time it took your printer to spit out the pages. Instead, choose Print Preview from the File menu before printing to save yourself the aggravation. You can change the margins from Print Preview if necessary. If more major formatting changes are necessary, press Esc to jump back to your document in the view you were in or double-click on the Print Preview document to jump out to Page Layout view. When things look right in Print Preview, you can choose the Print button to open the Print dialog box and then choose OK to start printing.

Make Copies

When something is important to you, *always* keep an extra copy in case you lose the original. Whether personal papers or computer files, *anything* can be damaged or misplaced. If a copy exists, however, you're protected even if the worst happens.

When a Copy Is Better Than the Original
You should use the copies you make of your software diskettes to install the program rather than using the original diskettes. That way, if your system eats a diskette, or otherwise destroys the data on the diskette, you've only lost a copy, not an original.

When protecting your computer files is the goal, your first priority is to copy your software programs themselves. As Chapter 4, "An Ounce of Prevention—Preparing a Word Survival Kit," exhorts in greater detail, always make copies of all your software *before* you install the programs on your system! Put these copies away in a safe place, preferably somewhere well *away* from your computer. That way, your software remains safe even if your computer melts down in a fire or gets stolen by a cat burglar.

Next, make backup copies of all your important data files as you work on them. Copy your data *frequently*. Whenever you work on an important file, save your work at least every 10 to 20 minutes (or often enough that you won't be too upset if you lose everything you've done since the last time you saved) and make copies every few hours (or even more frequently, see the rule for how often to save) on a separate diskette. This ensures that you always retain a relatively up-to-date copy of your work, even if your system experiences a severe data loss.

A Last Word on Avoiding Bad Things

Using Word can be easy and fun when done correctly. Just as in any other activity, however, if you do something wrong, you pay for it. The main idea to keep firmly in mind when using Word for Windows is to *be careful*! Follow this advice faithfully, and you can prevent most problems from occurring long before you need to worry about fixing them.

Speaking of prevention, the next chapter, "An Ounce of Prevention—Preparing a Word Survival Kit," gives you nearly everything you need to know to prepare yourself for any potential Word disaster.

An Ounce of Prevention—Preparing a Word for Windows Survival Kit

Most Word for Windows users sit around nonchalantly and wait for a computer disaster to strike. Then they moan and swear in the wake of catastrophe and do whatever comes to their fevered minds in a panicked attempt to recover as much salvageable data as possible—which isn't much.

But you're smarter than that, aren't you? (After all, you bought this book.) You'll do whatever you can to *prepare* for potential disaster so that the odds of recovering your valuable data are much higher than those for the typical unprepared computer user. It's like buying insurance: You invest a little time today to protect yourself should the unthinkable happen to Word for Windows and your data tomorrow.

Recovering from Accidents

The main way to be prepared for Word for Windows accidents is to have backup copies of *everything*. This way if something bad happens—something disappears from your hard disk, for instance—you can take your backup diskette files and copy them back to your hard disk.

Protecting Your Entire Hard Disk

You probably should get familiar with using the DOS BACKUP command. This command (as well as similar utilities from third-party manufacturers, such as Norton Backup and Central Point Backup) lets you back up huge volumes of data from your hard disk. Then, if you have a complete hard disk failure, you can restore your hard disk data from your backup diskettes. See *Oops! for Windows* for more information on backing up your Windows-based system.

What happens if you don't have backup copies? Well, life gets more difficult. Let's say you accidentally delete a file from your hard disk, and no backup copy exists. If you have DOS 5 or later, you can use the DOS UNDELETE command to bring erased files back from the dead. The command (issued after you exit Windows, from the DOS prompt), looks like

UNDELETE C:\DIRECTORY\FILENAME.EXT

You need to type the full directory path (where the file *was*) and the complete file name. If you can't remember the file name, issue this command

UNDELETE C:\DIRECTORY*.*

DOS lists every deleted file in the specified directory, and prompts you before it undeletes each one. When you find the specific file you just deleted, press **Y** and DOS does the rest.

You Need To File an Extension

When you're looking for Word for Windows files, remember that document files have .DOC extensions.

But you really don't want to use this clunky old DOS command if you don't have to. So read ahead and find out what you need to create a complete Word for Windows survival kit!

The Word for Windows Survival Kit

The best way to avoid using the UNDELETE command or manually rekeying all your data is to have backups of everything that's important. When you're dealing with Word for Windows, there are four things that are important: your original Word for Windows diskettes, copies of those diskettes, backup copies of all your Word for Windows data files, and all your program documentation and Que books. When you gather all these together, put them in a safe place in case the worst happens, and you accidentally lose your important files.

If you do lose your files, recovery is simple. If you lose data files, simply copy the backup files from your diskettes to your hard disk. (If you're not sure how to do this, consult a DOS or Windows manual or ask a computer guru.) If you lose your main Word for Windows files, you need to reinstall Word for Win-

> ### It's Better To Use a Copy
>
> It's always better to use copies of your program diskettes rather than the original diskettes themselves. If something goes wrong during installation, you still have your original diskettes in usable condition.

dows from the copies of your original Word for Windows diskettes. If these copies are unusable, you can always use your original Word for Windows diskettes.

Your Original Word for Windows Diskettes

You should always hold on to your entire original software package. Don't use the original diskettes for installation, however; use the DOS DISKCOPY command to make copies of these original diskettes.

Copies of Your Word for Windows Diskettes

To make copies of your original program diskettes, use the DOS DISKCOPY command. From the DOS prompt, type this command:

DISKCOPY A: A:

If your diskettes are 3.5" diskettes (used in drive B:), use this version of the command:

DISKCOPY B: B:

DOS asks you to insert the original diskettes, remove the originals, insert the destination diskettes (the copies), and (in most cases) re-insert the originals and destination diskettes several times. (This is because a certain amount of system memory is necessary to copy a complete diskette, and some swapping in and out is a matter of course.)

When you have the copies completed, label them and put them with the rest of your Word for Windows survival kit. If you ever need to reinstall Word for Windows, use these diskettes.

Backups of Your Word for Windows Data Files

It's a good idea to make backup copies of all your important Word for Windows files. I recommend creating a special directory on your hard disk to store all your Word for Windows document files so that you can easily copy the entire contents of the directory to diskette.

Let's say you named your data directory WORD-DOC, on drive C:. To copy every Word for Windows file in this directory to a 3.5" diskette, type the following command at the DOS prompt:

COPY C:\WORD-DOC*.DOC B:

Of course, you can do this from the Windows File Manager, as well. Just open the File Manager, highlight all the files in this directory, pull down the File menu, and choose the Copy option. When the Copy dialog box appears, type the letter of the drive you're copying to, and then press OK.

If you accidentally erase one of your data files, it's an easy job (from either the DOS prompt or the Windows File Manager) to find a copy of that file on your backup diskette and copy it back to your hard drive.

When You Have Too Much To Copy. . .

What happens if your files take up more disk space than fits on a diskette? The best solution is to use the DOS BACKUP command; this copies the files in a compressed format that can be spread over multiple diskettes. The only drawback to this method is that you just can't COPY the diskettes' contents back to your hard disk; you have to use the DOS RESTORE command to translate the files back to their native format. Pick up a copy of *Oops! What To Do When Things Go Wrong* for more information on the DOS BACKUP command.

All Your Documentation and Que Books

Naturally, you want to keep all your documentation in a safe place. And, even more naturally, you want to put all your Que books there, as well. (Unless, of course, you're actually *using* the book, in which case it's spread open next to your computer right now!)

What To Do When the Worst Happens

So, now that you have your Word for Windows survival kit, what do you do when the worst happens—and you actually lose your Word for Windows files? Read on to the next chapter to find out how to handle this kind of emergency!

What To Do When the Worst Happens

What's the worst thing that's ever happened to you? Been thrown in a jail cell with a guy nicknamed Killer? Had a flat tire in a driving thunderstorm? Drank some spoiled milk?

Well, all of these pale next to the bad things that can happen to you when using Word for Windows. Read on to find out the worst that can happen and how to deal with it.

What Is the Worst That Can Happen?

Let's take a poll. What do you think is the worst thing that can happen when using Word for Windows? Choose from one of the following:

1. Word for Windows breaks your computer.

2. Word for Windows destroys itself.

3. Your computer freezes up while you're in the middle of an important operation.

4. Something happens and you lose all your data files.

If you chose number 1 or 2, you don't have anything to worry about. It's just about impossible for Word for Windows to do any damage to your computer system and just as unlikely that Word for Windows will implode and destroy its own files. Now that you know these calamities are highly unlikely, anything else that happens won't look so bad, eh?

However, if you chose number 3 or 4, you're right on the money. Both of these instances can and do occur from time to time. Fortunately, they're both relatively easy to deal with, especially if you keep regular backup copies of your Word for Windows data files, as recommended back in Chapter 4.

What To Do When Your Computer Freezes Up

Sometimes, for no good reason, your computer freezes up. No matter what you do, no matter what key you hit or how frenetically you move your mouse, nothing happens. Nada. Zip. Dead city.

First, Unfreeze It

Make sure that it's not just Word for Windows that's frozen.

Press **Alt+Tab**. This key combination normally switches you from one Windows application to another. If this works, your computer is fine, but Word for Windows is screwed up. You need to *warm boot* Word for Windows. Switch *back* to Word for Windows and, if it's still locked up, press **Ctrl+Alt+Del**. Press Enter, and Word for Windows closes down. Now close down any other

> ## Be Patient. . .
>
> Don't get too eager to reboot Windows or Word for Windows. It's possible that nothing is frozen; your system may just be extremely slow. So organize your pens, shuffle the papers on your desk, and then try Word for Windows again. Don't wait more than one or two minutes, though. By that time, you can be sure that your system is really frozen!

open applications, exit Windows, and reboot your computer. You should be able to reenter Windows and restart Word for Windows.

If you *can't* switch to any other Windows applications, your entire system is frozen.

Press **Ctrl+Alt+Del** to reboot your entire system. (You may have to press these keys twice because Windows 3.1 has a fancy kind of protection system built-in.) If your system is so frozen that this key combination doesn't even work, turn your system off and back on from the reset button or the main on/off switch. This method is called a *cold boot*.

Next, Figure Out What Went Wrong

It is usually hard to figure out what you did to cause your system to ice up. You may have typed so many characters so fast that you overloaded the keyboard buffer (you speed demon!), or you may have tried to execute some forbidden sequence of commands. Even if you can remember the exact sequence of events and re-create them, the computer may not freeze up again. Computers are like that sometimes.

Of course, most freeze-ups aren't your fault at all. When you're dealing with Windows, the most common causes of frozen systems are low memory or lack of disk space. Windows is a hog about using both system memory and hard disk space, and if you have too little of either, Windows can get petulant and just refuse to work. You may need to increase the amount of memory and/or disk space on your system or just try running fewer programs at one time. (The latter is a good idea if you get frequent freeze-ups because some Windows programs can run into memory conflicts when run simultaneously.)

Finally, Get Back on the Horse

Okay, you're out of Windows and at the DOS prompt and have rebooted your entire system. (Make sure you remove your data disk before you reboot.) When your system restarts, restart Windows by typing **WIN** at the DOS prompt. When Windows is running again, relaunch Word for Windows, and load up the document you were using when the system went down.

If you're lucky, you saved this document right before the system froze. But then, who's ever that lucky? More than likely, you didn't save the document for awhile, and what you see on-screen is a prior version of the document, without any of your recent changes.

You can save yourself from this heartache by making sure Word for Windows' automatic save feature is activated. To enable auto save, choose Options from the Tools pull-down menu and select the Save category. Be sure that there is an x in the Automatic Save Every check box, and that the number in the text box is between 10 and 20. If your system freezes with auto save enabled, Word for Windows recovers your document when you restart the program.

If this feature *wasn't* enabled when your system froze, you're in deep trouble. The only thing to do is to rekey everything you changed or added since your last save. That's life!

What To Do When Your Data Is Lost

If your data files do get scrambled or erased, what can you do? The first thing to try is the DOS UNDELETE command. As explained back in Chapter 4, this command can bring erased files back from the dead.

All you have to do is exit Windows (or access the DOS prompt from within Windows). From the DOS prompt, type the following line

> UNDELETE C:\DIRECTORY\FILENAME.EXT

where you use the actual directory path and file name for the file that's gone. If you're lucky, this command will bring your file back from the dead. Of course, this command only works with files that were deleted, not with files that were scrambled. And it only works until the space used by the file is overwritten by a newer file, so use it right when you realize your data is gone. (Plus, it only works with DOS 5 or later, so if you have an older version of DOS, you're out of luck!) You can also undelete files with third-party programs such as Norton Utilities or PC Tools.

Of course, if you have a backup copy of your data files in your Word for Windows survival kit (see Chapter 4), you're safe. Just use the DOS COPY command (or the Windows File Manager) to find the file on your backup diskette and copy it back to your hard disk.

Does Your Data Get Damaged?

It's highly unlikely that a frozen system will damage your data. If it happens, however, you must start from scratch. (Of course, you also have to start from scratch if you hadn't yet saved the document on-screen at the time of the freeze.)

Can You Ever Lose Word for Windows Itself?

I know I said earlier in this chapter that Word for Windows just couldn't delete itself— and it can't, that I know of. However, *you* can accidentally delete Word for Windows files, just as you can accidentally delete any files on your hard disk. If this happens, use your copies of the original Word for Windows program diskettes in your Word for Windows survival kit to reinstall Word for Windows from scratch.

The Last Word on "The Worst"

Fortunately, Word for Windows is a fairly safe program, and relatively few catastrophic things can go wrong with it. When they do, though, it's enough to cause a nun to curse. But there's no sense getting high blood pressure about it, because once the damage is done, it's done. Follow the suggestions in this chapter on how to recover from these disasters, and you'll be up and running again in no time.

This the end of Part I. You now know everything you need to know to prepare for and prevent Word for Windows problems from occurring. If they do occur, though, you'll need all the help you can get. If you're experiencing a Word for Windows problem, turn to Section II to figure out what went wrong— and how to fix it!

Figuring Out What Went Wrong

Word for Windows Won't Start

You've had days like this: You're all ready for a heavy session of cruising with Word for Windows, you lean forward in your chair, position your hand over the mouse, double-click on the Microsoft Word program icon, and then—*nothing happens!* Before you panic, read this chapter. In it, I show you what can go wrong when you try to start Word for Windows and what you can do to get Word for Windows up and running.

Before You Can Start, You Have To Install

Before you can start Word for Windows, you have to have Word for Windows installed on your system. The initial installation of Word for Windows is done via the Word Setup Program found on the Setup disk (disk #1).

To install Word for Windows, you first have to have Windows up and running. (If you're not even this far, close this book, hop in your car, drive to your local book retailer, and buy a copy of *Oops! for Windows*. You probably need it.)

To run the Word Setup program, place the Setup diskette in drive A, pull down the File menu in the Windows Program Manager, and choose the Run option. When the Run dialog box appears, type the following in the Command Line text box:

A:SETUP

If your Setup diskette is in drive B, you need to type:

B:SETUP

The Word Setup program starts and asks you a few questions. The questions aren't hard (no calculus or essay questions!), so answer them to the best of your ability. When Word for Windows presents you with a dialog box asking what type of installation you want, click on Complete Installation so all the program files will be installed. The Setup program then starts installing the Word for Windows files and modifying your system files to maximize Word for Windows operations. You're asked to insert new diskettes from time to time as the setup continues. At the end of the installation, the Setup program creates a Word for Windows program group, complete with Word program and setup icons. When Setup is complete, you receive an on-screen message stating so.

The Right Way(s) To Start Word for Windows

Okay, Word for Windows is now installed—and properly so, if you answered all the installation questions correctly. Actually, Word for Windows does most of the work as far as getting configured to your system. Because all Windows applications share the same resources (printer drivers, video drivers, etc.) getting the right configuration for your system is fairly automatic.

So now all you need to do is start the program. Thanks to Windows' infinite variety, there are three key ways you can start Word for Windows.

> ### Read the README File
>
> After you install Word for Windows, be sure to read all the documentation, including the README.DOC file that is installed in the WINWORD directory. (This file is a standard Word for Windows file, so you can open it and read it in Word for Windows.) This file includes last-minute instructions, bug fixes, and other information too timely to be included in the printed documentation. It's extremely important that you take the time to read it.

Starting from the Program Icon

When you installed Word for Windows, the Setup program created a new program group called Word for Windows 2.0. (Imaginative, eh?) Open this program group by double-clicking on its icon (found in the Windows Program Manager). When the program group is open, you see icons for Microsoft Word and Word Setup. To launch Word for Windows, find the program icon labeled Microsoft Word and double-click on it or click once on the icon and choose Open from the File menu. Presto, change-o, Word for Windows is up and running.

Starting from the File Manager

If you prefer not to muck about with those silly little icons, you can also start Word for Windows from the Windows File Manager. Just open the File Manager (by double-clicking on the File Manager icon in the Windows Program Manager), and then scroll through the directory tree until you find the WINWORD directory. Highlight this directory, and then turn your attention to the file listing on the right half of the File Manager window.

Starting on Startup

You can set up Windows to start Word for Windows (and any other programs you use regularly) automatically whenever Windows itself is started. To have Windows start programs automatically, copy the Microsoft Word program icon into the Startup program group. Any program residing in the Startup group automatically loads whenever Windows starts up.

Find the file labeled WINWORD.EXE and double-click on it. Voila! Word for Windows is up and running!

Launching from a File

You can also start Word for Windows with a specific file already loaded. Instead of double-clicking on the WINWORD.EXE file in the File Manager, find the desired .DOC document file and double-click on it. Because Windows *associates* data files with their appropriate program files, opening a Word for Windows document causes Windows to launch the Word for Windows program as well.

Starting from the Run Command

The third method of starting Word for Windows appeals to users who remain faithful to command lines from the world of DOS. From the Windows Program Manager, pull down the File menu and choose the Run option. When the Run dialog box appears, type the following in the Command Line box:

C:\WINWORD\WINWORD

Hey, look—Word for Windows is up and running!

What Can Go Wrong When You're Getting Started

The most common problem when starting Word for Windows is that the proper directory path for the program file (WINWORD.EXE) is not specified. Remember, if Windows can't find the file, it can't start the program. So whether you're using the program icon method, the File Manager method, or the Run command method, make sure that Windows knows where to look for the Word for Windows program file.

> ### If You Can't Find It, Browse!
>
> If you can't remember the program name to type into the Command Line box, you can always press the **Browse** button and search through the directory tree and file list until you find the file you want.

If the right path is specified and Word for Windows still won't run, you probably have a problem with system resources. Chances are, for some reason, Windows doesn't have enough free memory to run Word for Windows. It's also possible that Windows may not have enough free disk space, either. Word for Windows needs all the resources it can get to run properly, so you may have to close down some other applications or add more memory to your system to run Word for Windows to the max.

Starting To Solve Problems When Starting

Now that you know how to start Word for Windows and what can go wrong when it starts, let's look at how to fix those darned starting problems.

10 Do's and Don'ts When Launching Word for Windows

1. **Do** make sure that Word for Windows is installed and set up properly for your system.

2. **Don't** expect Word for Windows to set itself up properly without your input; it only knows as much about your system as you tell it.

3. **Do** make sure that you have enough memory on your system to run Word for Windows; 2M is okay, but 4M or more is much better.

4. **Don't** install Word for Windows without first making copies of your Word for Windows program disks.

5. **Do** upgrade to Word for Windows Version 2.0c if you're using a previous version (and make sure you're running Windows 3.1, too!).

6. **Don't** be too quick to blame the hardware or software if Word for Windows doesn't start. First be sure you're doing everything right.

7. **Do** reboot the computer and try again if at first you don't succeed and the computer freezes up.

8. **Don't** feel ashamed to consult a Que book (such as *Easy Word for Windows* or *Using Word for Windows 2,* Special Edition) for more detailed information about how to use Word for Windows.

9. **Do** keep the original program diskettes—and their copies—in a safe place.

10. **Don't** forget to specify the full and correct directory path for the WINWORD.EXE program file.

Problem 1:

You can't start Word for Windows from the Program icon

Every program icon has a set of *properties* that allow it to find and start the program it represents. Among these properties is a simple listing of directory path and program name, otherwise referred to as the *Command Line*. If these properties are not configured properly, your program doesn't start. Period.

So, if you're trying to start Word for Windows from the Microsoft Word program icon, be sure the icon's properties are configured correctly. Especially make sure that the Command Line is set to include the full (and correct) directory path and program name for Word for Windows. (This is normally

> **Don't Forget To Browse**
>
> Remember, if you're not sure of the complete directory path for Word for Windows, you can always locate the file using the Browse button in the Properties dialog box.

C:\WINWORD\WINWORD.EXE.) To do this, click on the Microsoft Word program icon, pull down the File menu in the Program Manager, and choose the Properties option. Review the program's configuration to ensure that it's correct, make any changes that are necessary, and then close the dialog box.

If this solution doesn't fix your startup problem, skip ahead to Problem 5.

Problem 2:

You can't start Word for Windows from the File Manager

First, make sure you've located the right directory. By default, Word for Windows is installed in the WINWORD directory on drive C. During the installation, however, you can specify any other directory you want to use as the Word for Windows directory; if you did this, you need to locate that directory in order to start Word for Windows.

When you locate the directory, highlight it in the directory tree. Now you can start scrolling through the file listing (in the right half of the window) to find the WINWORD.EXE file. When you find the file, all you have to do is double-click on the file name, and Word for Windows should start. If it doesn't, jump ahead to Problem 5.

Problem 3:
You can't start Word for Windows from the Run command

This method of starting Word for Windows is deceptively simple. First, you have to open the Run dialog box (by pulling down the File menu in the Program Manager and choosing the Run option). Next, you have to enter the full and correct directory path and program name in the Command Line box. (This is normally C:\WINWORD\WINWORD.) If you installed Word for Windows into a different directory or onto a different hard disk, you need to type that drive and directory path into the box.

If you can't remember where Word for Windows is installed, click on the Browse button to display the Browse dialog box. This dialog box works a little like the File Manager, letting you scroll through a directory tree and file list to find the WINWORD.EXE file.

Once the correct directory path and file name are entered into the Command Line box, all you have to do is click on OK to start Word for Windows. If this doesn't work, move ahead to Problem 5.

Problem 4:
You try to start Word for Windows by double-clicking on a document file name, but nothing happens

You're supposed to be able to start Word for Windows by double-clicking on any Word for Windows document file name in the File Manager. (By default, document file names have .DOC extensions.) This procedure works because Windows *associates* data file names with their program file counterparts. If, for some reason, Windows has *not* associated .DOC data files with the WINWORD.EXE program file, then this feature doesn't work, and Word for Windows doesn't start.

To fix the problem, you have to associate the file name with the program file. Begin by opening the Windows File Manager (located in the Main group in Program Manager). Now pull down the File menu and choose the Associate option. When the Associate dialog box appears, type DOC into the Files with Extension box. If Windows has already associated the files, the text Word Document appears in the Associate With box. If not, you have to do the association.

Click on the Browse button to display the Browse dialog box. Now find the WINWORD directory and choose the WINWORD.EXE file. Click OK to close the Browse dialog box, and you'll find the correct directory path and file name inserted into the Associate With box. Click OK to close the Associate dialog box, and your files are associated. (It doesn't hurt at this point to quit and then restart Windows, just to be sure that your changes are permanently logged into the system files.)

If you still have problems starting Word for Windows, it's time to turn to Problem 5.

Problem 5:
Word for Windows tries to start, then quits or freezes

First, if your system freezes during Word for Windows' startup, you need to restart your system by pressing **Ctrl+Alt+Del**. If Windows 3.1 was running, it presents you with the following message:

> This Windows application has stopped responding to the system.
>
> * Press Esc to cancel and return to Windows.

```
* Press Enter to close this application that is not
responding. You will lose any unsaved information in
this application.

* Press Ctrl+Alt+Del again to restart your computer.
You will lose any unsaved information in all
applications.
```

If you press **Ctrl+Alt+Del** again, your computer restarts. This approach may be the best if you suspect Windows itself is causing trouble. If the likely problem is Word for Windows, just press Enter to dump Word for Windows from your computer's memory. If these methods don't work, use the reset button on the front of your computer or the main on/off switch for your system to reboot your system.

Once your system is functional again, the first thing to check is whether your version of Word for Windows is compatible with the version of Windows you're running on your system. Word for Windows requires Windows 3.0 or higher. Furthermore, the very first versions of Word for Windows contained lots of nasty bugs that could wreak havoc on your system. My recommendation is to use the latest versions of Windows and Word for Windows. As of this writing, the latest version of Windows is 3.1 and the latest version of Word for Windows is 2.0c.

Even if you have everything configured properly, your computer system may not have enough free memory to run Word for Windows. Try closing other Windows applications (to free up some memory) before restarting Word for Windows. You may also need to close Windows completely and then restart Windows and Word for Windows to allocate the maximum amount of memory for Word for Windows.

Also, you may not have enough free disk space to run Word for Windows. Because Windows employs free disk space as extra memory on some systems, running out of disk space can cause your programs not to run. You may need to delete some unused files from your hard disk before you try restarting Word for Windows.

The last possibility is that, for some reason, one or more of your Word for Windows program files have been corrupted or erased from your hard drive. Although this is an unlikely occurrence, it can happen if you have to reboot your computer while in the middle of certain operations. The only fix to this problem is to reinstall Word for Windows from the copies of your original Word for Windows program diskettes, which you should have in your Word for Windows survival kit (discussed back in Chapter 4).

Problem 6:
You can't find the Word program icon

Normally, the Microsoft Word program icon is found in the Word for Windows 2.0 program group. If you can't find the Word for Windows 2.0 program group, it could be hidden behind some other window or icon. Or the Microsoft Word icon could be in a different program group, or the icon may have been accidentally deleted.

> **Two Is Not Better Than One**
>
> When you're starting Word for Windows, make sure you don't have another copy of Word for Windows *already running!* Windows lets you run more than one copy of Word for Windows at a time, but doing so may use more system resources than you have available. Press **Ctrl+Esc** to invoke the Task List and check what's running.

Even if the program icon is deleted, it doesn't necessarily mean that Word for Windows itself has been deleted. Word for Windows is probably just fine, sitting all by itself and lonely on your hard drive. You now need to find the program icon or create a new one so you can start that lonely little program.

To find the group, pull down the Window menu in the Program Manager. The menu should list the Word for Windows 2.0 group (you may need to click on More Windows to display additional group names). Click on the Word for Windows 2.0 group. If the group window appears, your problem is solved. Double-click on the Microsoft Word icon and you're on your way.

If the Microsoft Word icon doesn't appear, begin creating a new one by opening the program group where you want to locate the program icon. With the group open, pull down the File menu and choose the New option. When the New Program Object dialog box appears, be sure Program Item is selected and then click OK. Now the Program Item Properties dialog box appears. In the Description text box, type **Word for Windows 2.0**. In the Command Line text box, type **C:\WINWORD\WINWORD.EXE** (or use the Browse option to locate the proper Word for Windows directory). When you're finished, click OK and a new Word program icon is added to the selected program group. When you double-click on the icon, Word for Windows should launch just as it always did.

A Last Word on Starting Word for Windows

Nothing is more frustrating than trying to start a program and having it not start. I hope you found the solution to your problem in this chapter. The key thing to remember is that Windows has to know where to look for the Word for Windows program file. If you're not using the full or correct directory path, Word for Windows just doesn't start, no matter how many times you try. Get the path right, and chances are Word for Windows will start just fine!

You Have Editing Problems

Have you ever finished saving and closing a 10-page document, and realized you needed to add another paragraph in the middle of page five? When you open the file, your insertion point is at the top of the document. How do you get to page 5 quickly to make the edit? You'd wear out your finger hitting the down arrow key hundreds of times! There must be a better way to get around in a Word for Windows document. There is! Read on.

Finding Your Way around Word for Windows

If you spend a lot of time writing, you also spend a lot of time editing. I hate to be the bearer of bad news, but few of us are perfect and get our words right the first time. (We wouldn't need Word for Windows if we did; we could use the trusty old Selectric.)

To edit your document, your file needs to be on-screen, and you must move your insertion point to the spot where you want to insert, delete, or move some text. You can move the insertion point to any part of the document you can see by pointing to the new location and clicking the mouse.

How To Get from Here to There

You move around Word for Windows by scrolling with the keyboard or the scroll bars. You can scroll down one window (screenful of text) by clicking in the scroll bar below the scroll box. Move up a window by clicking in the scroll bar above the scroll box. You can also click on the up and down arrows at the top and bottom of the scroll bar to scroll a line at a time.

If you need to edit a middle part of the document, drag the scroll box to the middle of the scroll bar and you'll be in about the right spot. Use the mouse to move the I-beam to the location where you want to start typing and click the mouse to reposition the insertion point. This repositioning is very important because when you use the scroll bars to move around in the document, your insertion point stays where it was. You may be viewing a different part of the document after scrolling with the scroll bars, but if you just start typing, the new text will be in the wrong spot.

Now let's do some big moves. If you want to move to the bottom of your document so you can continue writing your masterpiece, press **Ctrl+End**. Zap! You're there. To get back to the top of the docu-

ment, press **Ctrl+Home**, and, like magic, your insertion point is at the very top of your document.

If you want to move the insertion point a few baby steps, the arrow keys will

> ### What Are Those Double Arrows?
>
> When you are in *page layout* view, the vertical scroll bar has two extra buttons, one with a double-arrow pointing up and another with a double-arrow pointing down. These buttons let you move to the top of the previous page or the bottom of the next page.

do the trick. The right and left arrow keys move the insertion point a character at a time to the right or left. The up and down arrow keys move the insertion point up or down a line at a time.

Getting to the beginning or end of a line is also a snap. Press **Home** to move the beginning of the line or **End** to jump to the end.

If you know the page number of the text you want to edit, press the Go To key (**F5**), type a page number, and press **Enter**. Before you

can say, "Paging Mr. Miller," your insertion point appears at the top of the specified page.

Got To Get You into My Text

If the editing you want to do requires inserting text into your document, simply position your inser-

> ### Get Back to Where You Once Belonged
>
> If you were in the middle of editing a document when you last saved and closed it and want to be able to return to where you left off when you next open the file, here's an easy way. When you first open the file, press **Shift+F5** (the Go Back key), and your insertion point instantly jumps to its last location from your previous editing session. Word for Windows keeps track of the last three insertion point positions for your current document. You can cycle through the last three insertion point positions by pressing **Shift+F5** until you land where you want.

tion point where you want the new text to begin and start typing. Your text is inserted without deleting the existing text, and every-thing is reformatted just perfectly. Well, okay, there are *a few* potential pitfalls. Check out the following section titled "What To Do When You're Stranded in a Word for Windows Jungle." If you need to start a new paragraph or create a blank line, press the **Enter** key.

The Terminator Keys

Maybe you need to get rid of some unwanted text instead of adding new verbiage. The fastest way to eradicate single characters is with the Delete and Backspace keys. Delete erases the character to the right of the insertion point. Backspace removes the character to the left of the insertion point. One isn't better than the other; it just depends on where your insertion point is at the time.

You can use the Delete and Backspace keys to remove a word (or part of a word) in one fell swoop. Pressing **Ctrl+Delete** erases from the insertion point to the end of the next word on the right. Pressing **Ctrl+Backspace** erases from the insertion point to the beginning of the previous word.

Please Make Your Selection

When you want to modify your text or delete more than a single word, you need to tell Word for Windows which text you want to edit by *selecting* it. Selecting text means highlighting it before doing something to it. Doing what, you ask? Almost anything. Here's a list of some of the things you can do with a selection:

- Delete it
- Move it
- Spell-check it
- Print it
- Change the appearance of the type (bold, italic, etc.)

To select text with the mouse, drag the mouse over it. That's it. Okay, there are some shortcuts. If you want to select a word, double-click on it. You can select a whole sentence by holding down the **Ctrl** key and clicking anywhere in the sentence.

You can select text with the keyboard by holding down the **Shift** key while pressing any of the arrow keys. You can even combine the Shift and arrow key method with the Crtl method. For example, **Shift+Ctrl+right arrow** selects from the insertion point to the next word.

> ### Belly Up to the Selection Bar
>
> For making larger selections, get to know the *selection bar*, an invisible vertical strip just to the left of your text. You can tell when you are in the selection bar area because your mouse pointer turns into an arrow pointing toward about two o'clock. In the selection bar, you can select an entire line by clicking next to it. Double-clicking selects the whole paragraph next to the pointer. If you want to select several paragraphs, double-click but don't release the mouse button at the end of the double-click. Drag up or down to select multiple paragraphs. Pressing Ctrl and clicking in the selection bar selects the entire document. After you make a selection, just tell Word for Windows what you want done with it.

Moving Can Be a Drag

One of the easiest ways to move text from one portion of your document to another is the *drag and drop* method. The procedure for dragging and dropping is simple. Just select the text you want to move, position the mouse pointer anywhere in the selection, and click and hold down the left mouse button. Now you can drag the pointer up or down to where you want the text moved, and release the mouse button.

Watch Your ¶'s and Que's

The paragraph symbol (¶) stores all the formatting information for the preceding paragraph. When editing, be careful not to delete the ¶ at the end of the paragraph accidentally. If you do, the text takes on the characteristics of the following paragraph on-screen.

The best way to ensure that you don't inadvertently delete one of these symbols is to be sure they are displayed at all times. If you can't see the ¶'s, click on the ¶ button on the Ribbon. You can also display or hide other special formatting symbols by pulling down the Tools menu and choosing Options. In the Options dialog box, choose the View category and check the desired boxes in the Nonprinting Characters section.

Un-doing the Deed

You can restore inadvertently deleted text (or reverse just about any editing operation) by pulling down the Edit menu and choosing Undo. Depending on what sort of editing you did, the menu might say Undo Edit Clear or Undo Edit Typing. You can even undo what you undid by choosing Undo Undo. However, Word for Windows can only undo the last thing you did. The instant you make a mistake—STOP—and use the Undo command. Even then, Undo can't *always* save you, so do be careful.

If you want more detailed information about your ¶'s, check out your Ques—specifically Que's *Using Word for Windows 2, Special Edition.*

Why Can't I Get There and Other Editing Problems

So what sorts of problems can interfere with your document editing? You name it! If you try to move to a specific page, but you're viewing your document in draft mode, you can end up at the wrong page. Pressing the Delete key when text is selected deletes the text, even if you didn't mean to. In fact, depending on your options settings, pressing any key replaces the selection. For example, pressing the letter **m** while text is selected replaces the selection with an m.

If you don't pay attention to the paragraph marks, you're destined to struggle with Word for Windows forever. You can even unintentionally replace existing text by hitting the **Insert** key, which puts you in the *overtype* mode (a dangerous place to be).

Entering new text immediately after scrolling with the scroll bar can put a damper on your document. If you don't reposition the insertion point, your text won't be where you want it. Just moving the I-beam won't do it. You've got to click the mouse to reposition the insertion point. And, of course, you can't get there if there's no there. A common error is to try to position the insertion point in a part of the document that hasn't been created yet. The insertion point simply won't go there.

What To Do When You're Stranded in a Word for Windows Jungle

There are so many potential editing problems that they can't all be covered here, but let's take a look at solutions to some of the most common ones.

Problem 1:
You can't seem to add text without replacing existing text

This problem is caused by typing in the overtype mode. You can tell you're in the overtype mode when you see OVR in the lower right portion of the status bar. It's always safer to stay in the default (insert) mode, which you can get back to by pressing the **Insert** key.

If you find that Word for Windows defaults to the overtype mode, you can change the default by choosing Options from the Tools menu and clicking on the General category. If there is an x in the Overtype Mode box, click in it to deselect it.

10 Do's and Don'ts for Editing

1. *Do* keep the paragraph (¶) symbols visible at all times so you don't accidentally delete one and wipe out your paragraph's formatting.

2. *Don't* do your editing in the overtype mode; if you do, you may inadvertently replace text that you want to keep. You can get in (or out) of the overtype mode by pressing the **Insert** key.

3. *Do* drag and drop with the mouse to move text easily from one part of the document to another.

4. *Don't* do anything else before undoing a mistake. Word for Windows' Undo feature only keeps track of the last action you took.

5. *Do* use the scroll bars to reposition your view of the document.

6. *Don't* use the scroll bars to reposition the insertion point—it doesn't work. You need to click in the document or use the keyboard to reposition the insertion point.

7. *Do* use keyboard shortcuts to speed navigation. You can save time if you don't move your hands off the keyboard unnecessarily.

8. *Don't* forget to read on-screen messages, including the status bar, to clue you in on where you are and what you're doing.

9. *Do* use the selection bar to the left of your text to select large portions of text.

10. *Don't* be embarrassed if you need to seek additional help with your editing tasks. On-line help, the user's guide, and the many terrific Que books that cover Word for Windows in greater depth are all valuable resources.

Problem 2:

When you start a new paragraph, it doesn't have the characteristics you expect

Formatting problems are covered later in the book. For now, let's look at what to do when you want to insert a new paragraph between two paragraphs that have different formatting characteristics.

Overtype Won't Undo

Another big problem with the overtype mode is that when you delete text by typing over it, you can't Undo the deletion. If you stay in the insert mode and replace selected text, Undo works like a charm.

If you want the paragraph to take on the characteristics of the following paragraph, position the insertion point at the start of that paragraph and press the **Enter** key. (Press it twice if you want a blank line between paragraphs.) Now press the **up arrow** key to position the insertion point on the line where the new paragraph is to start and begin typing.

If you want the new paragraph to have the same attributes as the preceding paragraph, position the insertion point at the end of that paragraph, press the **Enter** key once or twice, and start typing the new paragraph.

If you add text in the middle of an existing paragraph, it looks the same as its surrounding text.

Of course, all these operations are easier to tackle with the paragraph symbols in view.

Problem 3:

Word for Windows doesn't properly keep track of what page you're on

This problem could have one of a couple of causes, so there are a couple of solutions. First, if you're in Draft view, Word for Windows doesn't display many text attributes or any font size changes. Therefore, Word for Windows can't accurately calculate what page it's on. The simple remedy for this situation is not to work in Draft view. Pull down the View menu and choose Draft to toggle Draft view off if there's a check mark next to it.

Another possible cause for this problem is that you don't have Background Repagination selected. Pull down the Tools menu and choose Options. In the Options dialog box, click on the General category, and then click in the Background Repagination box to activate it.

Repaginate Later

If you want to coax as much performance out of your system as possible, you may be better off not having Word for Windows perform background repagination. Background repagination uses a good deal of your computer's calculating power and can noticeably slow some systems down. Even if you don't have background repagination checked, Word for Windows repaginates properly when you print. You can also repaginate any time by choosing Repaginate Now from the Tools menu.

Problem 4:

You have trouble selecting the right text with the mouse

Don't feel alone. Many new mousers have trouble with this clicking and dragging stuff. Getting the mouse pointer to just the right spot to begin the selection, and then dragging just far enough to select exactly what you want takes a bit of practice. You may make a selection and find you've selected everything you want except that *one last character*. What to do? You could start the whole selection process over and try to get it right this time. Nah, too much work. Or you could use the keyboard to extend your selection. If you dragged from left to right to select several words and need to include a few more characters or words in the selection, hold down the **Shift** key and press the **right arrow** key or hold down the **Shift** key and click in the new location. With each click of the right arrow, your selection is extended one character to the right.

Problem 5:

You can't find the part of the document you need to edit

You remember the phrase you're looking for, but you can't remember where it is. Is it in the middle of page 8 or page 18? Even with Word for Windows' many document-navigation techniques, it can take way too long to find it by visually scanning your document. If you don't even know the general location of the text you want to edit, going to a specific page or using the scroll bars won't help much. Wouldn't it be great if you could search for the phrase you want and have Word for Windows jump right to it? Well, you can.

Choose Find from the Edit menu to display the Find dialog box. Type the characters you want Word for Windows to search for in the Find What text box. You can also specify whether Word for Windows should search backward (up) or forward (down) and whether the search should match only whole words and be sensitive to capital and lowercase letters.

> ### Cool Selection Shortcut
>
> You can use the *extension* key to select a word, sentence, paragraph, or the entire document. The extension key is F8. With your insertion point where you want it, press F8 once to turn on the extension mode (EXT appears in the status bar). You may now use the arrow keys to extend the selection or (this is the cool part) press F8 again to select the entire word, press it twice to select the sentence, three times for the paragraph, and four times for the entire document. If you pressed F8 one too many times, press Shift+F8 to reduce the selection by one step. When you want to get out of the extension mode, press Esc. The selection will still be selected, but the status bar won't say EXT.

If you have several instances of text that you need to replace with other text, such as replacing every occurrence of Dan Quayle with Al Gore, use the Replace command on the Edit menu. Type **Dan Quayle** in the Find What box and **Al Gore** in the Replace With box, and then click on Replace All. Replace gives you the same options as Find and lets you replace just certain occurrences of a word or phrase by clicking on Find Next, and then clicking Replace to make the switch or Find Next, to leave the original text and move on to the next occurrence.

Problem 6:
Your selected text won't go away when you type new text

Normally, when text is selected, any new text you type replaces the entire selection. If this isn't happening, chances are you accidentally turned off the Typing Replaces Selection option in the General category under Options on the Tools menu. If that's the case, just go back in and choose that option again.

You may have turned that option off because you were worried that you might unintentionally delete some text by selecting it and then typing something. There's no need to be *too* worried. If you do delete some text you meant to keep, you can always use Undo (on the Edit menu)—as long as that's the very next action you take.

Problem 7:
The new text you type isn't normal

When you add some new text in the middle of an existing paragraph, the new text takes on the attributes of the preceding text. If you position the insertion point just past some bold text, for example, the new text you type will also be bold. If you position the insertion point just before the bold text, and the preceding text isn't bold, the new text won't be bold.

If you must position the insertion point past some text whose attributes you don't want for your new text, remove the attributes before you start typing the new text. If you want to turn off bold, click on the bold button on the toolbar. If you want to turn off multiple attributes and type normal text, press Ctrl+space bar. If you've already typed a lot of text before you realize it's not right, you can select it and then remove the unwanted attributes.

Problem 8:
The wrong pages are changed when you use page setup

You'd think that when you make a margin, size, or orientation change on a particular page, only that page would be affected. Word for Windows doesn't work like that. When you pull down the Format menu and choose Page Setup, you need to specify which *section(s)* of the document you want to apply the changes to. If you don't have any text selected, your choices are This Section, This Point Forward, or Whole Document. If you selected text before summoning the Page Setup dialog box, your choices are Selected Text and Whole Document. If you have inserted section breaks, you also have a choice of applying the changes to Selected Sections.

Don't let all this section talk throw you. Sections are just Word's way of organizing documents for some types of formatting changes, such as page setup and columns. Word for Windows automatically inserts section breaks if you choose to apply your page setup changes to This Point Forward or Selected Text. Otherwise, the changes are applied to the specified sections.

A Final Word on Editing

You'll no doubt run into more than your share of editing bugaboos while using Word for Windows. Understanding the basic editing concepts and knowing some of the most common problems and how to avoid them may make your editing life easier. Don't panic (sound familiar?), and remember that you can Undo almost any editing mishap.

Your File Is Missing

CHAPTER
EIGHT

Every document you create in Word for Windows is stored in a file. If you don't know how Word for Windows deals with files, you're destined to lose them, and I can't think of a faster way to ruin a day than to lose an important file.

This chapter reviews some file management basics and explains how to use the Find File command to track down your missing files. It also explains how to solve other problems you may have while trying to manage those unruly files.

How Files Are Filed

Before you start trying to solve your file problems, you may want to read this short overview of files and file stuff. Ready? Let's begin...

Just What Is a File Anyway?

A file is a bunch of data. The data in a file can be a Word document, a worksheet from a spreadsheet program, or an image from a graphics program. The data in a file can even be the executable code that makes up a complete software program. (If you were to view the contents of a program file, they would look like gibberish to you, but your computer understands it without any trouble.)

Every file on your system has a name. (If a file didn't have a name, Windows and DOS wouldn't know how to find it!) A file name consists of three parts: an eight character (maximum) name, a period (optional), and a three-character (optional, maximum) extension. A typical file name looks like the following:

FILENAME.EXT

To use a file, you must use its complete and correct file name, and you must specify exactly where that file is on your system. Windows and DOS need to know which disk drive contains the file and in which directory the file resides. This information is called the file's path.

If you're not sure about all this path and directory stuff, read the next section.

And What's a Directory?

Files are stored on your disk in directories. A *directory* is like a hanging file in the file cabinet in your office. But unlike a hanging file, a directory is infinitely expandable, up to the available space on its disk. Directories can contain both files and additional directories, called *subdirectories*. Think of subdirectories as file folders that you'd put into hanging files. Other than the fact that subdirectories are located in other directories, there is no difference between directories and subdirectories. The main directory on your disk is called the *root directory* because it is like the root of a tree from which other directories branch.

When you specify a directory (while opening a file in Word for Windows, for example), you must use its entire *path*. The path is a list of all directories and subdirectories leading to a specific directory and file. You specify the path of the root directory on your hard drive as:

C:\

You specify the path of directory DIR01 off the root directory as:

C:\DIR01

And you specify the path of subdirectory DIR02 off directory DIR01 as:

C:\DIR01\DIR02

When you include the file name with the path, it looks like this:

C:\DIR01\DIR02\FILENAME.EXT

What's a Good Name for Your File?

By default, Word for Windows attaches a .DOC extension to all your files, unless you assign an alternative extension. The Open dialog box automatically lists files with a .DOC extension. At least at first, I recommend letting Word for Windows use

If you're using mostly files with an extension other than .DOC, you can change the default extension by editing the WIN.INI file. (Before you start messing around with the WIN.INI file, however, be sure you have your backup disk handy in case something should go wrong!) Display the WIN.INI file by pulling down the Tools menu and choosing Options. Press Ctrl+End to highlight WIN.INI, and then press Tab three times, so the Option text box is highlighted, and type DOC-extension. Press Tab once more to highlight the contents of the Setting text box and type your new default extension (.let, for example). Finally, click on Set and then Close to accept the changes.

its default extension. If you only use one extension, .DOC is as good as any. As you become more comfortable working with Word for Windows, you may find it practical to adopt the file naming tradition of using different extensions to signify different types of documents.

For example, you might choose to use a .LTR extension for letters, a .RPT for reports, and perhaps .CIA for those confidential documents. You can use these or any other extensions by simply typing them in when saving a file. If you want to let Word for Windows stick a .DOC on your file, you don't have to enter any extension.

Summary Information

When you're working with a large number of files or sharing files over a network, an eight-character file name (even with different three-character extensions) may not be flexible enough. Never fear, you can enter additional information about a document in its Summary Info dialog box. The Summary Info dialog box automatically appears the first time you save a file, after you enter a name in the Save As dialog box and click OK.

Summary. . . Be Gone!

If you don't need the extra file information that Summary Info provides, you can tell Word for Windows to stop nagging you for it when you save your files by pulling down the Tools menu and choosing Options. Then click on the Save Category and click in the Prompt for Summary Info check box to toggle the option off.

When the Summary Info dialog box appears, the Author text box is already filled in with the name you used when you installed Word for Windows. You can, of course, enter a different author name. You can also enter a title, subject, keywords, and comments. All of these items are optional, but, if you want to be able to search for files that meet certain criteria in any of these categories, you must fill them in.

Open Sesame

To open a file, pull down the File menu and select Open, or click on the Open button (second from the left) on the toolbar. Unless you changed the default file extension, the entry in the File Name text box is *.DOC and all the files in the list have a .DOC extension. You can type the name of the desired file in the text box or scroll through the list of files and click on the file you want. If the file you want doesn't appear in the list, you may need to change drives or directories. If you don't know about directories, you need to read *Oops! for Windows.*

Find File to the Rescue

If you've tried to locate your file through the Open dialog box and you still can't find it, what do you do? Lucky for you, Word for Windows has an incredible feature that simply won't *let* you lose a file. If you know anything at all about the file, the Find File command can find it for you.

You can access Find File directly from the File menu or through the Find File button in the Open dialog box. In the Find File dialog box, you'll see the path that was searched, how the files were sorted, a list of files, and, depending on previously determined criteria, the contents of the file.

If you need to search further, click on (surprise!) the Search button to invoke the Search dialog box. There are dozens of ways you can customize the search. I won't cover all of them—I'll just show you the slickest.

The File Name text box displays *.DOC (or whatever your default extension is). This means that when you execute the search, only files that have a .DOC extension are found. The Location section of the dialog box allows you to specify where Word for Windows conducts its search.

The default is Path Only, and the default path is normally
C:\WINWORD. If you want Word for Windows to search other drives
or directories, click on the Edit Path button and edit the path. You
can add more directories by separating each with a semicolon. The
following example would have Word for Windows search in the
WINWORD and the MYFILES directories on drive C:

C:\WINWORD;C:\MYFILES

Searching for Text in All the Wrong Places. . .

What if you didn't create (or don't remember) summary
information? If you remember at least a phrase that is
unique to the file, type that phrase in the Any Text text
box. You can also narrow the search by specifying a range
of creation or saved dates so Word for Windows only
finds files that match the other criteria and that were
created or saved between those dates.

You want to narrow the search
as much as you can so Word for
Windows will only find files
that are likely to be the ones
you want. If you've added summary information to your files
(and you remember what it
was!), enter that information
into the appropriate text boxes.
For example, if you know the
subject of the file you're looking for is Letters to Senators, type that
in the Subject text box.

When you have all the search criteria entered the way you want it,
click on Start Search. Word for Windows searches for the specified
files using the criteria you selected and returns a list of found files.
Pretty neat, eh?

What Can Go Wrong with Your Files

What *can't* go wrong with your files? Don't get paranoid, but this is
one area where Murphy's Law definitely seems to apply. The two
most common problems you may encounter while working with files
are misplaced files and damaged files.

Misplaced files can be the most frustrating because you know the file
is there...but where? You can forget which disk or directory contains

the file, or you can forget the file's name altogether. Maybe the file really *isn't* there after all. Perhaps you accidentally deleted it, you devil you.

Files become damaged. Sometimes your computer just decides to scramble a file for no apparent reason. Or possibly you are trying to use a file that was created in another program, and Word for Windows hiccups when you try to open the file.

What To Do When You Can't Find Your Files

Okay, now that you're a file expert, let's go fix some file problems!

Problem 1:

The file you want doesn't appear in the Open dialog box

Often the problem is as simple as having the wrong parameters in the File Name text box or having the wrong directory selected. If the File Name text box says *.DOC, but you saved your file with an extension of .RPT, it won't show up in the list. To correct the situation, replace the .DOC with the proper extension and click on OK.

If the wrong directory is selected, select the right one. If C:\WINWORD is the selected directory, but your file is in the C:\MYFILES directory, move up one branch on the directory tree (to the root directory) and then back down to C:\MYFILES. Do this by double-clicking on C:\ at the top of the directories list, and then scroll down to MYFILES and double-click on it.

Note that Word for Windows also remembers previously entered text in the dialog box. Check each text area carefully to be sure that it isn't looking for yesterday's info.

10 Do's and Don'ts of Good File Management

1. *Do* use a consistent file naming scheme so it will be easier to find files that belong to a certain category later.

2. *Don't* abuse your diskettes. If you want your files to remain safely on them, they shouldn't be exposed to temperature extremes, stored in proximity to magnetic fields (like paper clips), or used as frisbees.

3. *Do* use different file name extensions to categorize groups of files.

4. *Don't* store more files in a single directory than you can quickly scroll through.

5. *Do* create directories and subdirectories to organize your files.

6. *Don't* forget to check the author name to be sure Word for Windows knows who you are and can assign the proper author to your files.

7. *Do* fill in the summary information for your files to make it easier to locate them quickly later.

8. *Don't* use Find File if you know the name and directory of the file you're looking for. In that case, it's quicker to find the file through the Open dialog box.

9. *Do* use Find File to locate files based on criteria other than the file name or to have Word for Windows search multiple drives or directories.

10. *Don't* have Word for Windows search for text with the Any Text feature, except as a last resort. This is the slowest search method, but it's sure handy to have around when you need it.

Problem 2:
You have the right criteria and directory selected, but the file *still* isn't there

The file may have been accidentally deleted. If it was deleted, you may be able to undelete it with the UNDELETE command or a third-party utility such as Norton Utilities or PC Tools, discussed in Chapter 4.

Problem 3:
You know the file is there, but you can't remember its name or location

This is a very common occurrence for people in my age range (15 to 85). Memory lapses are the number one cause of file losses. Thank goodness for the Find File feature. Use the Find File feature, as described earlier in the chapter, to search any number of directories for the errant files.

Problem 4:
You've found the file you want, but it won't open!

Chances are you have too many other document windows already open. Word for Windows can only accommodate a maximum of nine simultaneous document windows. There are some legitimate reasons for having several documents open at once (but *nine?*). Most of the time, however, when you end up with nine open documents, it happens accidentally. You probably forgot to close some documents as you opened new ones. Or you may have tried to open multiple files from Find File when there were already too many files open. The solution to the problem is to close some of the open documents and try again.

The other possible cause is that you have too little available memory. Closing some files may help here. You may also need to close other applications you have running. If neither of these methods works, you might try closing all your applications, exiting Windows, and starting over. It sounds extreme, but sometimes this is the only way to free up sufficient memory.

Problem 5:
Your files really are missing

If the hard disk drive where your files are located is damaged, all the knowledge in the world about Word for Windows won't help. At this point, your only salvation is to have a recent set of backup diskettes or tapes so you can restore your files after your computer is repaired. You do have a recent backup, don't you? If not, go to the back of the class and then reread Chapter 4.

Problem 6:
You accidentally deleted a file

You want to kick yourself, don't you? You accidentally deleted a file, and you're getting that sinking feeling. Once again, the solution is a recent set of backups. You can also use the Undelete command in DOS or one of the third-party utility programs. For information on undeleting files, check out Chapter 9.

Problem 7:
A file created by another program won't open

Perhaps an associate asked you to edit a file created by some other program, but Word for Windows just refuses to open it. Several things could account for this problem.

Although Word for Windows can import (convert into Word for Windows format) files created by most of the major programs, it doesn't recognize everything. If the file was created in a program that isn't on speaking terms with Word for Windows, you will likely have a problem opening the file. In this case, if you have access to the program the file was created in, you may be able to use that program to export the file to a format Word for Windows does understand. Check out the documentation for the other program for export details.

Another problem could be that, even though Word for Windows can import files from recent versions of the other program, it doesn't know what to do with the file created by the Stone Age version of the program. One solution here might be to upgrade to a newer version of the other program or, once again, see if you can use the old version to export the file to something Word for Windows understands.

If the other program won't export in an appropriate format for Word for Windows to import, you might need to turn to a third-party conversion program such as WordPort from Advanced Computer Innovations, Inc. Third-party programs generally support far more file formats than standard applications do.

Problem 8:
A file created by another program imports, but the formatting is all messed up

Word for Windows does a pretty good job of converting basic formatting features, but other features used in other programs such as styles, tables, equations, and paragraph numbering may not survive the translation process.

There aren't many satisfactory solutions for this problem. If you do a lot of this sort of importing, you need to learn which features in the other program don't convert properly and avoid them. Another solution is to try a third-party conversion program. In addition to supporting far more formats, third-party conversion programs often translate more features than the conversion utility built into Word for Windows.

Problem 9:
The file looks like a bunch of gibberish

You open a file and there's garbage on your screen! It's not just that the formatting is a little off. The whole thing is messed up. This is probably another file import problem. In this case, Word for Windows probably made the assumption that the file was created by a specific program when it was created by another.

When you try to open a file that wasn't created in Word for Windows, the Convert dialog box prompts you to convert the file from the highlighted format. Word for Windows does its best to figure out what format to convert from, but it can make mistakes. If the highlighted format isn't correct, highlight the correct one. If there isn't a correct format, reread problem 7.

Problem 10:
When you save a file to another format, the other program can't use it

Well, technically this isn't Word for Windows' problem. That other darn program should import it. If you need to save a file in another format, you pull down the File menu, choose Save As, and then use the Save File as Type drop-down list to specify which format to use for the file. The same things can go wrong here as when you're importing a file. Perhaps the version of the other program is too old. For example, Word for Windows only supports WordPerfect versions 5.0 and 5.1. If you need to use the file with an older version of WordPerfect, you're out of luck. Of course, you can try one of those nifty third-party conversion utilities, or have Word for Windows export the file to a format that the older version of the other program can import.

A Last Word on File Management

File management is mostly common sense. Working with a lot of files does require some organizational skills (oh no!), but anyone can master the basics. If you think about what you're doing and are careful, you won't have any file management problems you can't handle.

What To Do When...

Your Text Takes a Vacation

You know you're not having a good day when your text takes a vacation. You're happily entering text on your Word for Windows screen and poof! some of your text disappears. Before you get too panicky, read this chapter. I guarantee I can improve your day!

How Word Handles Deleted Text

You add text to your document one character at a time—no matter how fast you type. When you want to add text, you just move your insertion point where you want the new text and type it. Darned straightforward, isn't it?

Of course, you can remove text one character at a time, too. You can also remove text in large chunks such as a whole sentence or the entire document (which can be a real time-saver if you do it on purpose!).

To remove text, position the insertion point where you want to start deleting and press the Delete key to remove one character at a time to the right or the Backspace key to erase one character at a time to the left. Removing a large block of text is equally simple. Just select the unwanted text and press the Delete or Backspace key.

No Penalty for Clipping

Think of the Windows Clipboard as an area of memory that serves as a temporary storage space for text (or graphics) that has been cut or copied. But remember that the Clipboard stores only the last thing you cut or copied. The next time you cut or copy something, you lose the previous Clipboard data.

You can also use the Cut command to remove selected text from the screen and place it in the Windows Clipboard. You can *paste* data in the Clipboard somewhere else in the document; you can even paste it into another Word for Windows document or a document in another program.

Why Your Text Might Leave You

The main reason text disappears is that you pressed Delete, Backspace, or issued the Cut command. Maybe you used these commands on purpose, maybe you used them accidentally, but you probably used one of them and that caused your text to vanish.

Sometimes your text isn't really gone, it's just invisible. This can happen if you're working in outline view and you *collapse* some of the text so there are fewer levels. Word for Windows also has an option for hiding text, which you might have applied inadvertently.

Typing text in overtype mode is another way to make your text disappear. If you accidentally press the **Insert** key, Word for Windows switches to the overtype mode and any new text you type replaces existing text.

In short, the main cause of disappearing text is that you did something you shouldn't. I suppose that I should recommend that you take more care with your work, but that kind of sounds like nagging, so I won't do it.

What To Do When Text Takes a Holiday

If you use a little common sense, you can avoid unwanted data loss. Of course, if you always used common sense, almost nothing would ever go wrong, so I don't know how much comfort that is. Realize that problems do occur, but knowing how to enter and delete data and use the commands correctly makes things go a lot smoother.

Problem 1:
You accidentally deleted some text

First, *DON'T PANIC!* If you haven't performed any other action since you accidentally deleted the text, all you have to do is pull down the Edit menu and choose the Undo Edit Clear command. Surprise, your text is back where it was! Of course, if you *did* perform another operation, you can't use Undo, and you have to read Problems 2 and 3 for more instructions.

10 Do's and Don'ts To Avoid Traveling Text

1. *Do* save your documents early and often.

2. *Don't* paste, cut, or copy text onto selected text that you want to preserve.

3. *Do* use the Undo command immediately to reverse any mistakes you've made.

4. *Don't* collapse paragraphs in an outline if you still need to view them.

5. *Do* use the Zoom Page Width option (choose Zoom from the View menu) to view your lines of text so they don't scroll off the edge of the screen.

6. *Don't* use the overtype mode because you cannot retrieve any text you delete while in this mode.

7. *Do* use the Cut command to remove text if you intend to Paste it into another part of the document or into another document.

8. *Don't* use any of these methods to try to make the pile of work on your desk go away. It doesn't help. Try taking a vacation yourself. Yeah, that'll work.

9. *Do* think carefully when Word for Windows prompts you about an action; more often than not, Word for Windows tries to warn you when you're doing something potentially stupid.

10. *Don't* use the Hidden Text option unless you want to risk invisible text.

Problem 2:
You accidentally cut some text

Boy, if it wasn't for bad luck, you wouldn't have any luck at all! Fortunately, you can easily remedy this situation. Just make sure the insertion point is where you want to reinsert the text, and then pull down the Edit menu and choose the Paste option. Your document is now back the way it was.

Problem 3:
You accidentally deleted or cut some text, and you can't use Undo or Paste to get it back

Well, this *is* a problem! You must have performed another action or cut some other text after you made your big boo-boo. This problem can also occur if you use the overtype mode to type over some existing text. Unfortunately, there's no easy fix. In fact, there's really no fix at all. After you perform another action or cut other text, the deletion is no longer in your system's memory or on the Clipboard, which means you can't bring it back with either Undo or Paste. (And when you're typing in the overtype mode, you can't bring back any text you've typed over, ever!)

About the only options available at this point are to reenter the missing text or revert to a previously saved version of your document. Sorry. (Try not to make this mistake too often, okay?)

Problem 4:
You can't find a specific block of text that you know is there

Well, this problem can happen for a number of reasons. First, you may have deleted or cut the text in question. Try using the Undo or Paste commands to put things right.

More likely, you've simply *hidden* the text. This situation can happen in a couple of ways. If you're fumble-fingered (like I am) you may have accidentally pressed **Ctrl+H**, the command to hide text, when you were reaching for **Ctrl+J** to justify your text. If this happens to you, the first thing to do is click the ¶ button on the ribbon. This action causes the hidden text to materialize along with any other normally nonprinting characters, such as paragraph and tab marks. Next, if you really don't want the text to have the hidden attribute, select the text (you can tell which text is hidden by the underlines under each character) and press **Ctrl+H**.

Another way to "hide" text is to collapse some lower-level sections while in outline view. This can happen by double-clicking on the + next to an outline level that has some visible lower levels. The solution is to double-click on the + again or click the All button on the ribbon, and your text appears. Another fix for this problem is just to switch your view by choosing Normal or Page Layout from the View menu; all the text in your document emerges.

Problem 5:
You have garbage instead of normal text on your screen

You open a document that was just fine yesterday, and you have a screenful of FLCs (Funny Looking Characters). Well, this is one of those problems that usually isn't your fault. The cause is usually a damaged file, which can happen for a variety of reasons. Maybe a bad spot developed on your hard disk and corrupted the file. Files also get damaged from electrical surges. Unfortunately, this is another of those problems that can be tough to resolve. The best fix is to use the file from your most recent set of backup disks. (Aren't you glad you've been making those backups?)

You don't have a backup? Here's a trick that sometimes salvages a *partially* corrupted file. Only use this method as a last resort, because all the formatting, like fonts and other text attributes, is removed.

First, close the file that's causing the trouble. Now, open the Windows Write program (usually in the Accessories group). Pull down the File menu, choose the Open command, and instruct Write to open the faulty file. When the dialog box appears asking whether you want to convert the file to the Write format, click on the No Conversion button. That's right, *don't* convert the file. When the file opens, it still probably has most of the garbage characters that were so annoying, but, if you're lucky, most of your text is there as well. Delete the garbage and save the file. Hey, it's not a perfect solution, but it may save you from having to re-key a whole lot of text. You're welcome!

Problem 6:
The text isn't visible as you type it

You know you're typing something because you can hear the sound of your fingers on the keyboard, but absolutely nothing appears on-screen. The insertion point is moving as you type, but it almost seems as though the text you're typing is invisible. Well, color me confused! In fact, color probably is the problem. Chances are that the source of your problem is white type on a white background. You accidentally specified white text as the color option in the Character dialog box. Let me tell you, it's pretty tough to see white text on a white background.

> **Black is Black, I Want My Writing Back**
>
> If you want to leave your text white while you write, you can simply change the background color. Click on the Application Control menu and choose Run. Open the Control Panel and double-click on the Color icon. Now click on the Color Palette button, pull down the list of screen elements, and click on Window Background. Click on any of the colors (other than white, of course) in the Basic Colors group and then click OK.
>
> Bear in mind, however, that changing the Window Background color only changes the way your document looks on-screen, *not* how your printed document appears. You should also know that changing the colors affects most other Windows applications, so be prepared to change back if you don't like the results.

The solution is to change the white text back to something a little more visible, say, black. Just select the white type, pull down the Format menu, and choose Character to open the Character dialog box. Pull down the Color list and choose black or Auto to make your text reappear.

Problem 7:
Your text is obscured

This problem is sort of the reverse of the white-text-on-a-white-background problem and is usually created by applying shaded borders with a foreground or background color that is the same as the text (probably black).

If you have text that's hidden by a border shaded with black, select the shaded text, pull down the Format menu, and choose Border. Choose the Shading option, and this time, instead of choosing black as either the foreground or background color, choose Auto or a color that doesn't hide the text; or, if you don't have a color printer, choose a light enough pattern that your text will be visible on top of it. If you just want to get rid of all shading, choose the None option in the upper-left corner of the dialog box.

A Pattern of Deception

You can generally get a fairly good idea of how your document will look prior to printing by using either the Page Layout view or Print Preview. Text and even most graphics display adequately close enough to their printed output. One exception to this, unless you have an exceptionally high-resolution video system, is shading patterns. To see what your shading patterns will look like when you print your document, you have to print your document (drat!). Also, shading looks pretty bad on just about anything but a laser printer. Even then, you should set your printer's resolution to its highest level through the Print Setup dialog box, accessible from the File menu.

Problem 8:
You accidentally delete an important file

If you're running DOS 5 or DOS 6, you're safe. Immediately after deleting the file, do the following:

1. Press **Alt+Tab** to switch to the Program Manager and pull down the **F**ile menu and select **R**un.

2. When the Run dialog box appears, type the following into the Command Line text box:

   UNDELETE C:\PATH\FILENAME.EXT

   Make sure you list the entire directory path and complete file name of the deleted file.

3. Click OK or press **Enter** and DOS undeletes the file and returns you to Windows where you can switch back to Word and go happily about your business.

Sometimes (not often, thankfully) DOS can't undelete your file. If this is the case, DOS alerts you, and you're out of luck. If you aren't running DOS 5 or 6, you can use third-party utility programs, such as Norton Utilities, to undelete your files. Better still, be careful and don't accidentally delete the file in the first place.

A Last Word on Departed Text

Perform your deletions and other actions slowly and carefully, and pay attention to the screen while doing them, and you can back out of most text-endangering operations. If you save your work often as you go along and back up your documents regularly, you'll be prepared should your text meet an untimely tragedy.

Your Document Looks Funny On-Screen

CHAPTER
T E N

Funny-looking documents are no laughing matter. If you aren't getting an accurate representation (or any representation at all) of your document, it's awfully tough to create word processing works of art.

Terms like WYSIWYG, resolution, and video driver and how they relate to your display problems will no longer be a mystery. You'll also learn about different views and what to do when things don't look right.

It's All How You Look at It

WYSIWYG (What-You-See-Is-What-You-Get) is the Holy Grail of word processing. Since the very first word processors a couple of decades ago, programmers have struggled to provide users with the most accurate representation of the printed page they could put on a screen.

Windows is perhaps the biggest boon to bringing "true" WYSIWYG to personal computer users everywhere. Because Word for Windows' screen display is so intimately connected to Windows, a brief discussion of how Windows handles the display of video information (the stuff on the screen) is in order.

How Windows Displays Pictures

Windows is a very convenient operating environment. After you establish certain system-wide settings, such as video resolution, the settings stay the same for every Windows application. (In the DOS world, you have to set up tons of options for each program you run.) So when you set up your Windows video drivers, you're set for *all* your Windows programs.

I'd Like To Make a Resolution. . .

There are several display standards for video cards and monitors. Each standard displays text and graphics at a specified *resolution*. Resolution is measured in something called *pixels* (dots), which are counted for both the width and height of your screen. The most common resolution for Windows use is called *VGA*, which is 640 pixels wide by 480 pixels high.

Windows uses a video display driver to determine your screen resolution. This driver works like many other Windows drivers; it's simply a file that contains the essential information Windows needs to send correct video images to your system's video card. Many video drivers are unique to specific video cards and control resolution, the number of colors, and all other information necessary to display the proper picture.

You select the video driver for your system when you install Windows. If you need to change your video driver, you can do so from the Windows Setup program in the Main group of Program Manager.

If you're adding a new driver to your system, you may need to copy the new driver to your hard disk. Windows prompts you when such a copy is necessary.

In My View, You Need a New Perspective

You have Windows and Word for Windows set up so that they display clear pictures, but why doesn't Word for Windows display your pages *exactly* the way they look when they print? You need to consider the different views you can use for your Word for Windows documents. Each of the views has advantages...and limitations.

Dodge the Draft

You can use Draft mode in both Normal and Outline views. The problem with Draft mode is that your screen doesn't look anything like what will pop out of your printer. Any special character formatting appears as underlines. Line breaks and pagination aren't accurate. Draft mode does improve the performance of your system *slightly*, especially if you have a slower system. For most systems, however, this improvement is not worth the trade-off.

Normal Isn't

Gee, Normal view makes it sound like you see on-screen what you normally get when you print. Normal view does let you see your formatting changes, including fonts and graphics, but there are several Word for Windows features that Normal doesn't let you see. Multiple columns, for example, appear as one really long column. You also can't see where pictures and other graphic objects will be placed on the printed document.

Let's All Shout for Page Layout

The closest you can get to a reasonable facsimile of your printed page while still being able to edit your document is in the Page Layout view. But don't go thinking Page Layout is the solution to your WYSIWYG problems. Some things you can't even see in Page Layout view, such as lines between columns and line numbers.

Also, when you are in Page Layout view, you can't see the bottom of the previous page when you move to the top of the next page. You can only see one page at a time. For this reason, you may find it useful to alternate between Normal and Page Layout views.

Previews of Coming Attractions

> ## Preview Distortions
>
> If you have the wrong printer selected, or no printer selected at all, you get a less-than-accurate picture of your document in Print Preview (if you get any picture at all). Remember, Print Preview actually prints your document to the screen. Word for Windows uses your selected printer driver to accomplish this feat. So make sure you have the correct printer selected. Get the picture?

If you really want to see what your page will look like when it's printed, your best bet is Print Preview. When you use Print Preview, you are actually printing your document. Instead of printing it to your printer, however, you're printing it to the screen. This is a terrific time saver because you can troubleshoot at the computer instead of printing the document 15 million times. You can even adjust margins while in Print Preview.

Pagination Proclamation

In any of these views, Word for Windows can lose track of what page you are on. Normal (without Draft mode) and Page Layout views are the only two views that can show you accurate pagination, and they can do it only if Word for Windows is doing its job of repaginating when necessary.

To be sure Word for Windows is paginating automatically (the default setting), choose Options from the Tools menu. In the General category, click in the Background Repagination check box. If you are using a slower system and want to repaginate manually, choose Repaginate Now from the Tools menu when you want to see accurate pagination. Don't worry if you print without proper pagination; Word for Windows automatically repaginates before printing.

Why Word for Windows Can Sometimes Look Bad

Display problems are some of the most common Word for Windows problems, but they are also often the easiest to fix. Run through this list of potential causes of video problems and see whether any sound familiar.

- You may have the wrong video driver installed. This is probably the most common Windows video problem. Run the Windows Setup program and make sure you've selected the right driver for your video card.

- You may need a new video driver. Check with the manufacturer of your video card to make sure you have the latest version of the video driver. Older drivers may not work properly with newer versions of Windows or Word for Windows.

- You may have the wrong driver for your particular system. Some video cards come with drivers for several different resolutions. Remember, you can't use a high-resolution driver with a low-resolution monitor, no matter which video card is installed in your system.

- Your cables may be disconnected. Be sure the cable from your video card to your monitor is firmly connected, as is the power cable to your monitor.

- Your video card may be inserted wrong. Make sure your video card is firmly seated in its slot in your system unit.

- Your monitor may need adjusting. Most monitors have the same type of controls as TV sets (contrast, brightness, and so forth), which, if maladjusted, can severely affect your display.

- Your monitor or video card may be bad. You need repairs or a new monitor or a new card. Enough said.

- You may be trying to use printer fonts that don't have corresponding screen fonts. Either install the appropriate screen fonts, avoid using the printer fonts that don't have corresponding screen fonts, or get used to seeing a less-than-accurate view of your text.

- You may have chosen a view in Word for Windows that doesn't display on-screen the attributes you're expecting to see.

What To Do When Your Screen Looks Weird

When it comes time to monitor your monitor, look no further than the following list of display problems—and how to solve them.

Problem 1:
Your screen is blank

First, check the obvious stuff. Is your monitor connected to your system unit? Is your monitor connected to power? Is your monitor turned on? Are the controls on your monitor adjusted so that you can actually see a picture? Maybe your screen saver just kicked in; try moving the mouse.

Next, make sure you have video on your system *without* Windows. Press Alt+F4 and then press Enter to exit Windows. If your monitor is out all over, your problem is a monitor problem, a video card problem, or a DOS video driver problem. Check with your local technician (or the original *Oops!* book) for possible solutions.

10 Do's and Don'ts for Display Happiness

1. *Do* make sure you have the correct video driver selected in the Windows Setup program.

2. *Don't* try to run your video card at a higher resolution than your monitor can reproduce.

3. *Do* use a screen-saver program (such as the one that's included with Windows) to prevent phosphor burn-in. Screen savers prevent "ghost" images from appearing on your monitor when a static image is left on-screen too long. Besides, a screen saver looks neat!

4. *Don't* use a screen-saver program. Oh no! Not contradictory advice! Screen savers use some computer processing power and can slow down your system. (Especially if you are using a slower system.) Furthermore, modern VGA and SuperVGA monitors are much more resistant to phosphor burn-in than older color and monochrome monitors.

5. *Do* use matching screen and printer fonts. If you're using Windows 3.1, use TrueType or Adobe Type Manager fonts to make your life easier.

6. *Don't* use an outdated video driver for your system.

7. *Do* select the highest resolution that your card and monitor can produce and that is comfortable for you to view.

8. *Don't* forget to plug in your monitor, connect it to your system, and turn it on.

9. *Do* adjust the brightness and contrast of your monitor to obtain the best possible picture.

10. *Don't* edit complex documents in Draft mode because it's difficult to tell in this mode what attributes your text contains.

The most common Windows video problem is an incorrect video driver. If you chose a high-resolution driver but your system can't display that resolution, you get a blank screen or a screen with total garbage on it. Run the Windows Setup program (if necessary, from the DOS prompt with the installation diskettes) and choose a different video driver. When in doubt, choose the generic VGA driver; it works with the majority of systems.

Finally, you may not have the right driver installed on your hard disk. Check with the manufacturer of your video card to be sure you have the latest version of the video driver, and then follow the recommended installation procedure to get it on your hard disk. After you install it, run the Windows Setup program to select the new driver.

Problem 2:
Your screen display looks like garbage

The potential causes of this problem are numerous. Some of the more common causes are the following:

- You have a loose connection or a bad cable. Check all your connections and cables. Replace any bad cables.

- You're using the wrong video display driver. Run the Windows Setup program and check the driver you have installed.

- You're using an outdated video driver. Check with your video card's manufacturer to obtain the latest version of the video driver.

- You're using a screen saver that Windows doesn't like. Some screen savers leave garbage on-screen when you close them. Try disabling your screen saver to see whether that rectifies the problem. Check your screen saver's documentation for instructions.

- Windows isn't configured properly for your system. This often happens when Windows is transferred from another system. Try reinstalling Windows from the original installation diskettes. When you do a normal installation from the original diskettes, Windows recognizes what equipment you have and gives you the opportunity to make modifications if it guesses incorrectly.

Problem 3:

Your screen display looks too large or too small

This problem is almost always caused by installing the wrong video driver in Windows—probably a driver with an incorrect resolution for your system. Run the Windows Setup program and choose another driver.

Problem 4:

Your screen display flickers

Some high-resolution displays (1,024 x 768) use what is called *interlaced* display technology. An interlaced display lets you run higher resolutions on lower-cost hardware, but such a display sometimes results in a very annoying screen flicker. Your options are to buy a video card/monitor combination that can run in *non-interlaced* mode or to select a lower resolution, such as 800 x 600 or normal VGA (640 x 480).

You Have To Have a Good Memory To Get Good Video

When you're selecting video drivers in the Setup program, don't get carried away. Many drivers have options for various resolutions and color densities. Some of the higher resolutions (and higher color densities) are only available if you have an enhanced version of the card with additional video memory installed. Use the Setup program to select the right driver for your specific video card setup.

Just Your Type of Word for Windows Flicker

With higher resolution video drivers and scalable fonts, such as TrueType and ATM (Adobe Type Manager), you may notice that the line you're on flickers with each character you type. Newer video drivers often correct this problem, but you can usually correct it by sticking with the 800 x 600 or 640 x 480 drivers supplied with Windows 3.1.

Another factor to consider when trying to minimize flicker is the video card and monitor's maximum *vertical-refresh* rate. Most non-interlaced systems refresh (redraw) the screen at 60Hz (times per second). This rate is slow enough that people sensitive to flicker are bothered by it, particularly under certain lighting conditions. If you are really concerned about flicker, get a video system that can handle at least 70Hz refresh. Your eyes will thank you.

Problem 5:
Your fonts don't display properly

You may have the wrong fonts installed in Windows. Open Control Panel and double-click the Fonts icon. From here, check to make sure that you have the right fonts installed for your system. (You might try removing all the fonts and then reinstalling them one at a time.)

Bad On-Screen, Good on Paper

Although Word for Windows (and some other Windows applications) uses a special Small Fonts typeface for any small size (usually under 6 points) TrueType font on-screen, it always uses the correct font when you print your document.

If you're trying to view TrueType fonts at a very small type size, you may be disap-pointed. TrueType is not optimized for small type sizes, so Windows substitutes a plain, sans serif typeface for whatever TrueType font you selected below a specific size. This substitution makes for better legibility on-screen. Pull down the View menu, choose Zoom, and then choose 200% to see small sizes.

When using very small point sizes, you may also find that your lines of text extend past the right margin (and off the right edge of the screen). You can either use the horizontal scroll bar or pull down

the View menu, choose Zoom, and then click Page Width. Sometimes, even changing the Zoom to Page Width doesn't resolve the
situation. In that case, choose Options from the Tools menu, select
the View category, and click in the Line Breaks and Fonts as Printed
check box to toggle it off.

Also note that some fonts displayed at very large sizes look some-
what jagged on-screen. The degree of jaggedness depends in large
part on your screen resolution. Don't worry; the "jaggies" don't
affect how fonts are actually printed on paper.

Problem 6:
You can't find fonts you know are installed

This is a common problem with Word for Windows. You have a font
installed and yet you can't access it from Word for Windows. You
check your font setup and verify that the font is really installed, yet
it still doesn't show up in your application. What's the deal?

The deal is simple. You need to have a printer selected in Word for
Windows before it will display all your available fonts. Use Control
Panel to select a printer and make sure Windows knows which port
on your system it's connected to.

If your printer is installed in Windows, the problem could be that
Word for Windows doesn't know which printer you want to use.
Pull down the File menu, choose Print Setup, and select the correct
printer. If the correct printer is already selected, try selecting another
printer and then reselecting the correct printer. (I know this sounds
weird, but trust me.) All your fonts should now show up in Word for
Windows' font selection lists.

Problem 7:
You can't find your cursor

Most displays on laptop and other portable computers have trouble
tracking fast motion (like that of your mouse), so your pointer seems

to disappear when you're moving the mouse. Normally, the pointer reappears when you've finished moving the mouse. There are several solutions to this problem; one solution is to choose the Mouse icon in Control Panel, and then click on the Mouse Trails check box in the Mouse dialog box. Not all mice support Mouse Trails. If yours doesn't, the option won't be available in the Mouse dialog box. You also can slow down the mouse tracking speed using the scroll bar in the Mouse dialog box.

There are also third-party solutions for the disappearing pointer problem. Check with your software dealer for programs, such as Cursorific, that allow you to change the size and shape of the pointer.

Problem 8:
Your Windows screen colors make Windows unviewable

First, be sure you have your screen colors adjusted correctly. Open Control Panel and double-click on the Color icon. When the Color dialog box appears, pull down the Color Schemes list and choose a different color scheme. If *none* of the color schemes look right, you either have a defective video card or video driver, a dying monitor, or very strange taste. If things look okay outside of Windows (running DOS programs or just at the DOS prompt), it's probably the video driver. Check with your card's manufacturer for a replacement driver.

Problem 9:
Your text is gone!

You can tell your document is open; its name is on the title bar. But you can't see any text. Chances are, you've accidentally scrolled to a portion of the document that doesn't have any text. Check the scroll boxes in the scroll bars. If the scroll box in the vertical scroll bar is at the bottom, drag it up toward the top. If the scroll box in the horizontal scroll bar is at the right, drag it toward the left. Your text should now be visible.

Problem 10:
Text that was typed in multiple columns displays in one column

You told Word for Windows you wanted to type in 2 or 3 columns. When the program didn't protest, you figured everything was alright. But, as you typed your text, all you saw on-screen was one long narrow column of text. What's going on here? Relax, it's normal, literally. In Normal view, your columns don't display side by side. To see the multiple columns, pull down the View menu and select Page Layout. You can also see the multiple columns in Print Preview or, of course, when you print the document.

Problem 11:
You can't see the end of your lines of text

This problem is usually caused by setting the Zoom to a percentage that is too high, say 200%. Try zooming out to 100%. Pull down the View menu and select Zoom. Click on the 100% button and then click OK. If this doesn't do it, summon the Zoom dialog box again, but this time click on the Page Width button.

Problem 12:
Your fonts don't display properly and graphics don't display at all

You probably have Draft mode selected while in Normal or Outline view. Pull down the View menu and select Draft to toggle it off. You may *choose* to work in Draft mode because it allows your computer to work faster. Displaying fonts and graphics takes quite a bit of computer resources and can slow down scrolling and even typing on a slower computer. Turn on Draft mode by repeating the steps I just gave for turning it off. Draft mode doesn't affect what your printed document will look like.

Problem 13:
Pictures and other graphic elements don't appear where they should on the page

You must be in Page Layout view to accurately see the positioning of graphic elements. Pull down the View menu and select Page Layout to switch to the page layout view.

A Final Word on Display Issues

When you have your monitor up and running, make sure you have the brightness and contrast settings adjusted to a comfortable level, and that you're using a screen resolution that doesn't make you squint to see those really small characters.

Environmental factors can also play a large role in your viewing comfort. Glare is a huge problem and can be reduced by adjusting the lights near your computer, adding a glare screen, or perhaps something as simple as closing a window shade. Changing your viewing angle by adjusting your chair up or down can also help. If your system is set up right, you'll be more comfortable, and your Word for Windows session will be a lot more enjoyable.

What To Do When...

Your Printer Doesn't Print Right

CHAPTER ELEVEN

Your printer is one of the key parts of your computer system—and one that's often prone to problems. When you try to print from Word, you may encounter problems with Word for Windows itself, with Windows, with the fonts you've installed, or with your printer and associated hardware. The nice thing about a printer problem, however, is that it doesn't throw your entire system into jeopardy, as does a hard disk problem. You can always copy your document files to a diskette and take them to another PC with Word for Windows for printing.

How Word for Windows Talks to Your Printer

Word for Windows communicates with your printer through Windows. And Windows communicates with your printer via *printer drivers*. A printer driver is nothing more than a small file of instructions necessary for Windows to use the printer. Like all files, the printer driver is installed on your hard disk, and Windows must have the driver installed to communicate with your printer. If you use multiple printers, you use multiple printer drivers; if you add a new printer to your system, you must install a new printer driver.

Windows, being a nice, unified operating environment, also lets you globally specify printers and printer settings. You can also globally add more fonts to your system. This centralization through Windows saves much time and trouble and, in most cases, works pretty well.

Installing a New Printer

You add new printers by opening the Control Panel and double-clicking the Printers icon. When the Printers dialog box appears, a listing of currently installed printers also appears. To add a new printer, click on the Add button. The Printers dialog box expands to show a List of Printers. Scroll this list, select the printer you want to install, and then click on the Install button. (If your printer is not listed—which isn't likely—select Install Unlisted or Updated Printer from the list, click on Install, and follow the on-screen instructions from there.)

Setting Up a Printer

After the printer is installed, you can configure myriad options that affect the way your printer prints. After you click on the Setup button in the Printers dialog box, a dialog box of options specific to your selected printer appears on-screen.

Additional options may be available to you beyond the dialog box. Because each printer driver offers different options, I can't tell you exactly what you'll see. I can tell you that the default options are generally acceptable, although you may want to call in your resident PC pro to guide you through some of the more obscure features of your printer.

> ### Printer Setup in Word or Windows?
>
> The printer setup dialog boxes are available through Windows' Control Panel and through the File menu in Word for Windows. Whichever one you use will have the same effect on all your Windows programs. The normal convention is to do your initial setup when you first install a new printer, and when a printer is initially installed, you are in Windows' Control Panel. Also, some configuration options aren't available through Word for Windows' printer setup, such as changing ports.

Understanding the Print Manager

Windows includes a utility called the Print Manager that sends the file you want printed to a temporary area on your hard disk and then sends the file to the printer as the printer is able to receive the information. This process lets you get back to work on a document as soon as the file you want printed is sent to your hard disk, instead of waiting for the printer to print the whole thing. The catch is that using Print Manager can slow down the printing process just a bit. If you want to see how Print Manager affects printing performance, turn off the Use Print Manager option by clicking in the check box next to it in the Printers dialog box (which is accessed through the Control Panel).

> ### Printing by Default
>
> Although you may have multiple printers installed on your system, only one of these can be your main, or *default*, printer at any given time. The default printer is the printer that Word automatically uses for printing, unless instructed otherwise. To set a default printer, open the Print Setup dialog box by pulling down the File menu and choosing Print Setup. Double-click on the name of the printer you want to be the default. The selected printer is now the default printer for all Windows applications, just as if you had made the change through the Control Panel.

Adding Printer Fonts

Windows 3.1 incorporates TrueType font technology, which makes it easy to add new fonts that can be printed with good results on just about any printer.

To add new fonts to Windows, open the Control Panel and double-click the Fonts icon. (Note that you can't do this printer setup task from within Word.) The Fonts dialog box displays all installed fonts and a sample of the currently selected font. Click on the Add button to display the Add Fonts dialog box.

What's a Font?

A *font* is a specific combination of typeface and style. Each typeface has a name (such as Times New Roman) and can be printed in specific styles (such as italic). You generally want to use *serif fonts* (fonts that have those little decorations at the ends of the letters) for body text, and *sans serif fonts* (fonts without those little decorations) for headings. You don't want to use too many fonts in a single document because they make the page less readable and take more time to print.

From the Add Fonts dialog box, you must instruct Windows where to look for the new fonts. (If you're adding third-party fonts, chances are that they're on a diskette.) After you choose OK, Windows goes through the font installation procedure, during which you click OK a couple of times to install your new fonts to your hard disk and Windows. When you next access Word for Windows, or other Windows programs, the new fonts should show up in the font list boxes, along with all your previously installed fonts. If they don't, check out the Chapter 12, "Your Fonts Aren't Fontasizing."

Potential Printer Problems

Now that you have your printer drivers installed and your fonts loaded, what could possibly go wrong when you try to print from Word for Windows? Plenty, partner!

First, you may have the wrong printer driver installed. You may have selected the wrong driver for your printer, or the driver selected may be out-of-date. Various aspects of your printer setup may be incorrect. You also need to check your font setup because fonts themselves can cause perplexing problems if they're not installed correctly.

Second, you may not have enough disk space or memory to print. Make sure that you have plenty of both, because Windows needs all the space it can get to complete the printing operation. Also, make sure that you're not trying to print from a Windows application (such as Word for Windows) and a DOS program at the same time—it usually causes lots of grief.

Finally, you could have real printer hardware problems. These problems range from the mundane (you're out of paper, you forgot to turn on the printer, you have a bad connection) to the fairly serious (your printer is broken).

The bottom line is that you need to check a number of things, including both hardware and software, if you have problems printing in Word for Windows. If you do have printing problems, check out the Problems/Solutions section in this chapter.

Solving Your Printing Problems

You've worked all day on a massive document, complete with multiple fonts, lines, artwork, and other neat graphic elements. You lean back in your chair, click your mouse on the Print button, and...whoa, this thing isn't printing right! What do you do now? Read the following sections.

Problem 1:
You can't print at all

Although this is a common problem, it's seldom a Word for Windows problem. Check the following items.

10 Do's and Don'ts for Printing in Word for Windows

1. *Do* check all your printer's connections on a periodic basis; check the cables from your system unit to your printer and the power cable from the printer to the wall outlet.

2. *Don't* run out of paper in the middle of a print job, or Windows may give you an error message.

3. *Do* install the right driver for your printer.

4. *Don't* use outdated printer drivers; check with your printer's manufacturer (or with Microsoft) to get the latest version of your printer's printer driver.

5. *Do* keep your printer in a well-ventilated area, free from dust and cigarette smoke. Just ask the Surgeon General—second-hand smoke is a leading cause of premature printer problems.

6. *Don't* forget to turn on your printer before you start to print!

7. *Do* add whatever fonts are necessary for your desired output.

8. *Don't* add so many fonts that it takes a half hour to scroll through your fonts list.

9. *Do* make sure that you have the right printer selected as your default printer; remember that installing and selecting are two different things.

10. *Don't* forget to check all the options and settings for your specific printer; one little detail buried three dialog boxes down may cause you unhappiness at some point in your life.

1. Make sure that your printer has power. Is the power cable plugged into the printer and the power outlet? Is the printer turned on? Is the printer *on-line* (normally determined via a little button on the printer's front panel)? Does your printer have enough paper available? If the printer is connected correctly but you have no power, you have a printer problem. See your local printer repair center.

2. Is your printer connected to your system unit? Check both ends of the connection and then try a new cable. (Cables can wear out and break over time.) Is the printer attached to the correct port on your system unit? If all this checks out, it's time to look for software solutions to your problem, so move to Step 3.

3. Is the correct printer driver installed? Have you checked to see whether you have the latest version of your particular printer driver? If not, you need to install a new or different printer driver.

4. Is your printer set up correctly? Have you checked all the setup options? Have you checked the port assignment for your printer? If your setup is incorrect, you may not be able to print at all.

5. Do you have adequate free disk space? (Windows uses temporary disk space to store information while a print job is in process.) If not, you may need to delete some files before you attempt to print again.

6. Are you trying to print from both Word for Windows and a DOS program at the same time? This process generally doesn't work, so print from each program separately.

If none of the solutions presented solves your particular problem, you need to call in outside help. (Sorry.)

Problem 2:

Your printer driver doesn't work

First, make sure that you have the right printer driver selected. Next, be sure that you have the latest version of the printer driver. (When in doubt, use the driver that was shipped with your version of Windows, especially if you're using Windows 3.1.)

Keep in mind that some printers can emulate more than one printer, such as a PostScript printer. This capability can be built into the printer or added with a cartridge. If you've set your printer to emulate something other than itself, you can't use its normal driver—you need to use a driver for whatever printer your printer is now emulating or reset the printer to match your driver. Got that? Good.

Problem 3:

Your output is pure garbage

The most likely cause of this problem—believe it or not—is the cable connecting your printer to your system unit. If this cable is poorly connected, you can get the *strangest* printouts you've ever seen. Check each connector to make sure that it is firmly connected and that none of the connecting pins are bent or broken. Also, be sure that the cable itself is in good shape; after a few years of use, the wires inside these cables can become brittle, bent, or broken. When in doubt, change cables.

The next most likely cause of this problem is an incorrect or outdated printer driver. Check to make sure that you have the right (and the latest) driver for your particular printer.

Next, be sure that you have the same printer *selected* as you have hooked up to your machine. If you have multiple printer drivers installed, it's fairly easy to select the wrong one in the list. If Windows thinks it's printing to printer A, but printer B is hooked up to your system, who knows what will print out?

Make sure, too, that all your setup options are configured correctly. Incorrect settings can cause output problems.

If your printer gives you a solid black block on the paper (but no text) as output, your printer probably can't print reverse text (white on black). To solve the prob-

> ### Do as I Say, Not as I Do
>
> The day after I wrote the printing chapter for the original *Oops!* book, I tried to print out the chapter and received a page of garbage in response. Because I'm supposed to be an expert in these things, I spent the next hour installing new printer drivers and changing setup configurations, without affecting the resulting output. Finally, I remembered to check my cables, and—lo and behold!—one of the connectors had come loose. A quick push of the plug and my output was back to normal. Learn from my experience and *check your cables first!*

lem, use a graphic image. You can create graphic images with a variety of graphic programs, including the Paintbrush program that comes with Windows. Word for Windows also includes its own really cool drawing program called Microsoft Draw, which lets you insert reverse text graphic images.

Problem 4:
Windows freezes up while you're trying to print

This problem is generally caused by a lack of memory or a lack of disk space. To cure the former, close any other active applications before you initiate printing. To cure the latter, delete any unneeded files from your hard disk. In particular, clean out the TEMP directory; a Windows crash could have left some garbage files in this directory, which Windows uses to store temporary printing information. You must have at least 2M of free hard disk space for temporary printing information.

Problem 5:
Your output appears different from your screen

First and foremost, make sure the fonts you think you have are really installed. If in doubt, remove and then reinstall all your fonts.

If you use TrueType fonts with some printers (usually non-laser printers), you can get some pretty unusual printouts. You may find, for example, that all your TrueType fonts are double-spaced! If you experience these kinds of problems, try opening the Setup dialog box for your printer driver (from the Print Setup option in the File menu in Word for Windows) and selecting the Print TrueType as Graphics check box. Although this action may slow down your printing a tad, it can fix many TrueType printing anomalies.

Problem 6:
You can't print certain fonts

Again, be sure that you have the fonts installed because Word may try to use fonts that have long since been deleted. Also, make sure that your printer is capable of printing the fonts you've selected. You can't print PostScript fonts, for example, on a non-PostScript printer.

If you're trying to print Windows TrueType fonts on a PostScript printer, not all fonts will look good. This is a bug in TrueType itself and mainly affects types at very large point sizes. This happens because TrueType fonts have to be converted to PostScript format before they can be printed on a PostScript printer. The best solution is not to use TrueType fonts on your PostScript Printer, opting instead for PostScript fonts.

Type as Graphics—Or Is It Graphics as Type?

When you set up a printer, the Options dialog box gives you the option to Print TrueType as Graphics. For normal printing, don't select this option; it may slow down printing on some printers. However, this option is sometimes necessary if you experience weird TrueType printing problems, such as double-spacing where you should be getting single spacing.

TrueType fonts can cause quite a few printing "incidents," not the least of which is failure to print, mainly because TrueType is a memory-intensive technology. If you're trying (and I emphasize the word *trying*) to run Word for Windows on a system with only a couple of megabytes, you'll be lucky to get TrueType to work at all. (For that matter, you'll be lucky to get *Windows* to work at all!) Even if your system has a great deal of memory, including many different fonts in a single document can tax your available memory to its limits. Pack your system to the max with memory if you really want to take advantage of TrueType fonts.

Be aware also, that some fonts floating around are supposedly TrueType-compatible. Well, some are, and some aren't. The rule of thumb is that: the less you pay for your fonts, the less likely they are to work correctly. If you get them for free—well, do I need to draw you a picture?

Problem 7:
Only some of your pages print

If you're missing the last pages of a printout, they may still be in your printer's memory, waiting for a *form-feed* signal from Windows. This problem is fairly common (especially with laser printers) and indicates that something is awry with your printer setup. Your printer may just be out of paper, or a page may be physically stuck in the printer. Add paper, if necessary, or check the paper path to make sure the works are not totally gummed up and then try to print again.

Problem 8:
Your printed page looks half finished

If you're using a laser printer and trying to print a document that contains many graphics, you may find that your printer doesn't have enough memory to print the entire document. To solve this problem, pull down the

---

Don't Forget To Add Memory to Your Printer

Most laser printers, even expensive ones, don't come equipped with enough memory to print lots of graphics on a page at the highest resolution. The good news is that you can add additional memory to most laser printers. But, how much should you add? Because laser printers are *page printers*, they need to have enough memory to hold the entire page's image in memory at one time. A full page (8 1/2 x 11) graphic at 300dpi (dots per inch) requires about 1M. At 150dpi, you only need half that

continues

Don't Forget To Add Memory to Your Printer (continued)

amount of memory. Don't start jumping for joy because your printer came with 1M. Some of that memory is used to store fonts and other printer overhead tasks, often up to a half a megabyte. If your printer seems to have enough memory for all your fonts, adding one additional megabyte usually takes care of your graphic printing problems. Sometimes you can get 2M for just a few more dollars than the price of one—go on and splurge, you deserve it.

File menu and choose Print Setup. Highlight your printer in the list and click the Setup button to open the setup dialog box for your printer driver. Change the resolution from 300 dots per inch to 150 dots per inch. This action instructs Windows to send less graphic information to your printer, which, in turn, requires less printer memory to print the pages. The downside of this procedure is that the graphics in your printed document are less detailed than before, but a full page at low resolution is better than a partial page at high resolution, right?

Problem 9:
Your printer is slow

If you're annoyed by printer pokiness, try the following solutions:

1. Open Windows' Main program group and double-click the Print Manager icon. After the Print Manager window opens, pull down the Options menu and choose High Priority. This process gives your print jobs first priority when you perform multiple tasks in Windows.

2. Don't perform other tasks as you're printing. Your PC only has so many resources; using fewer of them speeds up your print jobs.

3. Turn off the Print TrueType as Graphics option in the Options dialog box in your printer setup. Printing graphics is slower than printing text. (This only helps with laser printers and others that have the memory to store downloadable fonts.)

4. Reduce the amount of graphics in your document. Again, printing graphics is slower than printing text.

5. Reduce your printer's resolution in your printer driver's setup dialog box. Lower resolution means Windows is sending less information and your printer has less to print.

6. Eliminate graphics at print time. When you're printing drafts of your document, you may not care if the graphics print at all. You just want to proofread the text. Pull down the File menu and choose Print. From Word's Print dialog box, click on the Options button and select Draft Output in the Printing Options area. Later, when you want your graphics to print, just repeat these steps to toggle off draft printing.

7. Turn off Use Print Manager from Windows' Printer dialog box. This action bypasses the Windows Print Manager and sends your print jobs directly to your printer, speeding up the process a bit. The downside of this action is that you have to wait until the print job is finished before you can get back to work in Word for Windows.

8. Use resident printer fonts instead of other fonts that have to be *downloaded* (sent from the computer to the printer) at print time. Many printers come with a nice selection of built-in fonts. If you choose fonts that are already in your printer, you'll save the time required to send them to the printer. If you want to use downloadable fonts, use TrueType fonts. On some machines, TrueType prints faster than ATM or PostScript. (This is not a universal truth; check it out on your system before you implement it as a printing strategy.)

9. Remove graphic displays but leave the boundaries by pulling down the Tools menu, choosing Options, and then selecting Show Text with Picture Placeholders.

10. If all else fails to speed things up, buy a faster computer or printer (or both!)—or learn to live with sloth.

Problem 10:
You can't load new fonts

Yes, Virginia, there is a limit to the number of fonts you can install in Windows. It isn't a limit based on the number of fonts, however, but a limit based on the complexity of the fonts that you are using. Based on an average font complexity, you probably can't load more than 300-400 fonts. (Of course, if you have this many fonts, it probably takes you half a day just to scroll through your font list!)

Problem 11:
You can't print from Word for Windows and another application at the same time

This problem is normally due to some sort of memory problem and generally manifests itself as printing conflicts. Printing from each program one at a time should fix things.

If you're trying to print from Word for Windows and a DOS application at the same time—*don't!* Windows doesn't do this well and generally just poops out and may even give you an error message. Print from one application at a time.

Problem 12:
You can't print while using a print-sharing device

Some offices use print-sharing devices to hook up multiple PCs to a single printer. (It's actually a kind of network without all the complicated network stuff.) Unfortunately, these devices don't always work reliably with Windows. If you're having trouble with your print-sharing device, try these solutions:

- Contact the device's manufacturer to make sure that you have the latest version of the support software. While you're talking to the manufacturer, check to see whether you need any sort of hardware upgrade to run your version of Windows.

- Click the Printers icon in Control Panel, and then click on the Connect button. After the Connect dialog box appears, turn off the Fast Printing Direct to Port option. This action can eliminate some problems.

- If all else fails, get rid of the print-sharing device. Doing so may be the easiest fix.

How *Do* I Share the Printer?

There are a number of reliable printer-sharing devices. ASP in Sunnyvale, CA makes some neat devices specifically designed for LaserJet printers. Because they don't use any external software, they work just great with Windows. There are also some reasonably priced networks that aren't *too* horribly complicated, which work well with Windows. Check out Lantastic from Artisoft. With a network, you have the added advantage of being able to share files, as well as the printer. You also might consider the increased productivity of *not* sharing printers at all. An inexpensive printer for each computer might be the way to go.

Problem 13:

Word for Windows doesn't print envelopes from the envelope feeder

When you try to print envelopes, Word for Windows prompts you to load an envelope even though there's a stack of envelopes in your printer's envelope feeder. Isn't this program smart enough to *know* where your envelopes are? Not until you tell it. When you install an envelope feeder on your printer, you need to make sure the option to print them from the feeder is selected. Pull down the Tools menu and select Options. Click on the Print category and then click the appropriate check box in the Envelope Options area.

Problem 14:

You can't remember how to print an envelope

With an address on-screen, pull down the Tools menu and select Create Envelope, or click on the envelope button on the toolbar. Word for Windows searches your document and grabs the address it thinks you want and places it in the Addressed To box of the Create Envelope dialog box. If Word for Windows guessed incorrectly, choose Cancel, select the address you want, and repeat the above steps for creating an envelope.

Problem 15:
There's no return address for your envelope

Word for Windows automatically prints a return address if the information has been entered in the User Info category (accessed by pulling down the Tools menu and choosing Options). If no return address appears, enter one in the Return Address box and answer yes when asked whether you want to save the new return address as the default mailing address. If you want to add or change the return address manually, pull down the Tools menu and select Options. Press the **down arrow** key 6 times to highlight the User Info category and enter your return address in the Mailing Address box the way you want it to appear on your envelopes. When you print your envelopes, you can eliminate the return address for that envelope by clicking in the Omit Return Address check box.

Problem 16:
You can't print just the envelope you've added to a document

After using Word for Windows' envelope feature and adding the envelope to the document, you want to print just the envelope, but when you tell Word for Windows to print just page one, the first page of the letter prints. What gives? When Word for Windows adds an envelope to the top of your document, it's page 0. To print just the envelope, pull down the File menu and select Print. Click in the From box in the Range section of the Print dialog box and type **p0**. Press **Tab** and type **p0** in the To box. Word for Windows prints from page 0 through page 0, which is just the envelope.

A Last Word on Printing Problems

In spite of the large number of potential causes, most printing problems are easily corrected. But, in your rush to check every single setting and driver, don't forget that your printer requires regular maintenance to stay in tip-top shape. Change your ribbon or toner regularly, clean the dirt and paper shavings from the inside of your printer. Be sure that all your cables are in good shape, and keep your printer away from dirt and smoke. If you do your job, your printer will do its job.

Your Fonts Aren't Fontasizing

CHAPTER TWELVE

If you didn't care how your documents looked, you probably wouldn't be using Word for Windows. One of the areas where Word for Windows shines brightest is the fantastic way it handles fonts. But, you need to understand how to deal with fonts effectively in Word for Windows to avoid a potential font *faux pas*.

In Chapter 11, I spent a lot of time discussing fonts and how they relate to the printing process. Fonts and their problems are such an important part of Word for Windows, however, that I decided that they needed their own chapter.

The Fontastic World of Fonts

The judicious use of fonts can turn an ordinary document into a message that cries out to be read and believed. The various typefaces and other attributes that make up your fonts can change the way your readers perceive what (and how) you write. One font can make your writing very formal and businesslike, another might convey elegance and prestige, and a third could make you feel warm and fuzzy all over.

Looking at Fonts

If you followed the advice in the preceding chapter, your fonts are installed and working properly in Word for Windows. If you're using TrueType or ATM(Adobe Type Manager) fonts, your screen fonts should closely match what comes out of your printer.

Making the Point

Type sizes are specified in *points,* which refer to the height of the characters. One point equals about 1/72 of an inch in height. You usually select large point sizes (14 points and up) for headlines and such and smaller point sizes (from 9 to 12 points) for body text.

Word for Windows helps you avoid picking the wrong fonts by showing you what you'll get before you get it. Pull down the Format menu and select the Character option. When the Character dialog box appears, you see a sample area that displays a preview of the selected font with any attributes you assign. Pretty neat, eh?

Choosing Fonts

To choose a font for text you are about to type, pull down the Format menu and choose Character. In the Character dialog box, click on the down arrow next to the Font drop-down list and select the desired font. (A sample of the font appears in the Sample area.) Change the point size and add any other attributes you desire.

When you close the dialog box, you'll be typing away with the new font. If you want to change the font for some text you've already typed, select the text and follow this procedure.

You can also choose fonts from the ribbon or with the keyboard. Until you're

> ### Keeping Things in Proportion
>
> Back in the not-so-good old days of typewriters (ugh!), each character occupied the same amount of horizontal space as every other character. Fonts of this type are known as *fixed-width* or *monospaced* fonts. Nowadays, most folks use *proportional fonts*. With proportional fonts, each character occupies the correct (or proportional) amount of horizontal space; an uppercase M, for example, takes up more space than a lowercase l.

very familiar with the different fonts you have available on your system, I recommend sticking with the Character dialog box because this method allows you to check out the look of various combinations before committing them to your document.

Fonts, along with other formatting options, can also be applied with the Word for Windows *style* feature. You can use Styles to format entire paragraphs only. Other than that limitation, styles have some really incredible advantages over the other methods. Check out Chapter 18 for more information about styles.

What Can Go Wrong with Fonts

The most common font problem is overuse. Using too many fonts in a document can cause all sorts of troubles—both technical and aesthetic. When in doubt, stick with one or, at most, two fonts in a document. It's all too easy to get that horrible "ransom note" look. Invest some time in learning the principles of good document design, including which fonts are best in various situations. Check out the problems section in this chapter for information about other common font problems.

10 Do's and Don'ts for Fonts

1. *Do* choose fonts from the Character dialog box so you can preview a sample of the font before applying it to your text.

2. *Don't* use too many fonts in a single document. If in doubt, use just one or two fonts.

3. *Do* change the default font to the font you use most often. Remember, you can include any attributes you like in these default changes.

4. *Don't* use fixed-width (monospaced) fonts, such as Courier, unless you want your documents to look like they came out of a typewriter...really ugly!

5. *Do* take the time to learn more about the whole subject of fonts and good document design.

6. *Don't* panic if you have fonts installed that Word for Windows can't find. Go back and reread the previous chapter for instructions on how to get your fonts to show up.

7. *Do* use the Replace command to change all your paragraphs with one set of fonts and formatting attributes to another. You can also use this method to replace characteristics for words or phrases within a paragraph.

8. *Don't* choose the Replace All option from the Replace dialog box unless you're very sure you want replace *every* occurrence. Instead, you can use the Find Next Replace option to confirm each replacement, one at a time.

9. *Do* save your file just before performing any sort of global action (such as Replace All) that can have devastating effects on your document.

10. *Don't* forget that fonts can greatly affect the way your document is perceived, so choose the right font for the occasion.

How Fonts Misbehave

You're typing away merrily, changing each of your headings to Arial 18-point italic with a 1/2-inch indent and then changing the body text for each paragraph to 12-point Times New Roman with no indent. Twenty pages later, your boss, client, or better judgment strongly suggests that you change the headings to Cloister Black 20-point with centered alignment. What do you do? Never fear, the answers lie ahead.

Problem 1:

Your screen fonts don't match your printed fonts

Chances are you're using screen fonts that don't have corresponding printer fonts. To get as close as possible to WYSIWYG (What-You-See-Is-What-You-Get), you must have matching screen and printer fonts. If you're using TrueType fonts, this problem is taken care of automatically. (You can tell when you choose a TrueType font because of the TT next to it in Word for Windows' font lists.) With some other kinds of fonts, you have to specify whether you want screen fonts installed. Check your font package's documentation or ask your dealer to be sure your screen and printer fonts are in sync.

Problem 2:

The font you normally use isn't the default font

It's a pain to tell Word for Windows to change the font every time you start creating a new document. Wouldn't it be great if Word for Windows just *knew* what font you normally used? You can make it happen.

> **I'm Okay, You're Okay, So What's Normal?**
>
> When you create a new document, its default settings are based on a *template*, which is sort of a pattern that contains all the information necessary to format your document. Unless you specify a different template, the default template is called *NORMAL.DOT*. If you change the
>
> *continues*

default font, the change affects the *normal style*, which is contained in the NORMAL template. A style is nothing more than a collection of formatting instructions which can be applied to a paragraph or group of paragraphs. (Chapter 18 deals with style problems.) A template can contain many styles, as well as a set of *macros* and *glossaries*. See Chapters 17 and 19 for more information on these devices.

To change the default font (along with any of its attributes), select the font and attributes you want as the new default in the Character dialog box, and then click on the Use as Default button. A dialog box appears asking whether you want to change the font for the Normal style to Lucida Bright at 12 point (or whatever). The dialog box also explains that the change will affect all new documents based on the NORMAL template. Choose Yes. Later, when you exit Word for Windows, one more dialog box appears, asking whether you want to save the global glossary and command changes. Answer Yes to record the new defaults.

Problem 3:
You can't remember how to change your font's size

This problem is very common. Remember that to change an attribute in Word for Windows, you usually need to first select the portion of the document you want to change and then tell Word for Windows what change you want to make.

To change the point size of some existing text, select the text, click on the down arrow for the point size list on the ribbon (just to the right of the font list on the ribbon) and then click on the point size you want. Here's a cool keyboard shortcut for changing the point size of a font. Each time you press Ctrl+F2, the size increases by one point. Ctrl+Shift+F2 decreases the size by one point.

Problem 4:

Your fonts won't change size when you select a new point size

You've selected a font and started typing, and then you decide you want to make the text larger. So you select the text and choose a different point size from the point size list on the ribbon or in the Character dialog box, but the font stubbornly remains the same size on-screen. How can this be?

The cause of this problem may be that you're using a printer font that doesn't have a matching screen font. (See Problem 1.) The most likely cause is that you're using a *non-scalable* font. Non-scalable fonts are fonts that are only available in a limited number of sizes (maybe only one). Most laser printers, for example, have at least two built-in non-scalable fonts, Courier and LinePrinter. If you've chosen a font that won't change size and you need to change size, the solution is simple: choose a different *scalable* font.

Problem 5:

You can't remember how to change non-contiguous sections of text from one font to another

Well, you *could* select each section, one at a time, and make the desired changes, but there's a better way. Word for Windows has a magical feature called *Replace*. All right, most word processing programs have a replace feature for replacing a word or phrase with another word or phrase. But Word for Windows can replace text and formatting characteristics.

> **Better Save Than Sorry**
>
> You know by now (because you've read the early chapters of the book) that you should be saving your work regularly. Well, whenever you are about to perform any action that has the potential of really messing up your entire document (such as any sort of Replace All activity), save your file FIRST! That way, if the Replace winds up replacing a bunch of good stuff with a ton of bad stuff (it *can* happen), you can always close the document and retrieve the version you just saved, and all will be right with the world.

To make the replacement from say, the Arial font to Cloister Black, pull down the Edit menu and choose the Replace option. The Replace dialog box appears on-screen with the insertion point in the Find What text box. Click on the Character button, pull down the Font list and choose Arial, and then click OK. Font Arial appears next to the word Format under the Find What box.

Now, click in the Replace With text box, select the Character button, choose Cloister Black, and click OK. To execute the replacement, click on the Replace All button and...Zap! All the headings that were Arial are now Cloister Black. If you do a replace by mistake, you can usually pull down the Edit menu and choose Undo Replace to reverse the action.

Problem 6:
The mysterious flickering fonts

This problem doesn't happen with every font or on every computer system. Of course, it happens on every computer I use! What happens is that, while I'm typing, the entire line of text I'm on flickers on and off (very annoying!). This problem doesn't affect the way the document prints, but it can drive you batty.

The folks at Microsoft don't have a sure cure for this problem, though each succeeding version of Word for Windows eliminates more bugs. Make sure you have the very latest version of the software (version 2.0c as of this writing), as well as the latest video drivers for your video card.

This problem is more prevalent at higher resolutions and generally goes away if you use Windows' generic VGA video driver, although this fix didn't work for me. This problem also seems to occur with some fonts more than others. For example, I get lots of flicker with a font called Bodoni, but not with Times New Roman. Gee, and Bodoni's a nice font.

The one sure way I've found to get rid of the problem is to switch to Draft mode, which you can only do from Normal or Outline view. The problem is, in Draft mode, you can't see what your fonts look like on-screen. Oh well. At least one of these methods should lessen your difficulty until Microsoft solves the problem once and for all.

Problem 7:
Your fonts appear as a bunch of strange (but cute) pictures

You picked Wingdings, didn't you? Windows 3.1 comes with a TrueType font called *Wingdings*, which isn't made up of normal characters. Instead, you get all kinds of little pictures and symbols. Another name for this sort of font is Dingbats.

This font can be very useful for adding interest to your documents (especially in bulleted lists), and they're fun! But not when you don't want them. To correct the problem, just select a not-so-dingy font. If you accidentally typed a bunch of

Wingdings Revealed—Yeee Ha!

If you're intrigued by these neat little pictures and you want to see what symbols are available to you, pull down the Insert menu and choose Symbol. Select Wingdings (or whatever symbol set you like) from the Symbols From drop-down list, and you'll see the available symbols. If you want to insert one at the insertion point, just double-click on it.

text with a Wingdings-type font selected, you don't need to retype the text. Just select the text and choose a different font. Your text now appears as real words.

Problem 8:

The fonts aren't right in a document that was created on another computer

If a document was created on another computer, it was formatted with the fonts available for that system. If those fonts aren't available on your system, Word for Windows makes a best guess as to what available fonts it should substitute. If Word for Windows guesses wrong, use the Replace command as discussed in Problem 5 to change to the fonts you want. If you bring in documents from other computers regularly, there is a way to tell Word for Windows which font substitutions to make for the incoming fonts. I'd recommend calling in your local PC guru for this job.

A Final Word on Fonts

Now that you know how to choose and use fonts, print out some sample pages of some of the fonts your system has available for future reference. Examine your printed pages with the eye of a designer and try to determine whether the look you've achieved best serves your purpose. Of course, substance is the most important thing in your documents, but nothing beats a good first impression.

What To Do When. . .

Your Columns Look More Like Snakes

CHAPTER THIRTEEN

Because Word for Windows is such an advanced word-processing program that integrates many elements from high-end desktop publishing programs (sounds like a plug from a press release, doesn't it?), it should be a breeze to create columns that are cleanly and neatly lined up. After all, what you see on-screen is *exactly* what you'll get when you print...right? Well, getting your columns to march to your tune requires an understanding of how columns work in Word for Windows and why they might just slither off to the beat of a different drummer.

How Word for Windows Lets You Line Up Your Text

Word for Windows provides several methods for formatting your text in columns. Choosing the right one can be baffling. If you need to create rows and columns of text and numbers, such as a list of employee names and phone numbers, you can use the tabs or the Table feature. (I cover the Table feature in Chapter 16.)

When you create rows and columns using tabs, you're creating a *tabular table*. For creating a professional-looking newsletter, Word for Windows' Columns feature is just the ticket.

More Than You Ever Wanted To Know About Tabs

Tabs are *not* the same thing as spaces. When you use proportional fonts, the space bar can leave you in a different position on each line, depending on the preceding text. Tab stops are set at specific distances from the left margin. When you press the **Tab** key, your insertion point moves to the right and stops at the next *tab stop*. To actually see your tab stops, click on the paragraph symbol in the toolbar.

Word for Windows has default tab stops (represented by upside-down T's on the ruler) every half inch, but you can set your own custom tab stops. The default tab stops may be acceptable for indenting the first line of a paragraph, but for almost anything more complex than that, you'll want to set custom tab stops.

The easiest way to set custom tab stops is with the ruler. To set a tab stop, just move the mouse pointer to the part of the bottom half of the ruler where you want to place the tab stop and click. As soon as you set a custom tab stop, all the default tab stops to the left of the custom tab stop disappear. For this reason, you generally need to set a custom tab stop every place you want a tab stop in your tabular table.

There are four kinds of tab alignment: left (the default), center, right, and decimal. With a left-aligned tab stop, the text flows from the tab stop position to the right. When you type text at a center-aligned tab stop, the text is centered at that spot. Your text flows from the tab stop to the left at a right-aligned tab stop. Decimal alignment is great for aligning columns of numbers with decimal points. At a decimal-aligned tab stop, the text (usually numbers) flows to the left until you press the decimal point (period). After you enter the decimal point, the text flows to the right so that all your numbers are lined up on the decimal point.

To set a custom tab stop with other than the default alignment, click on the tab button on the ribbon with the desired alignment and then click on the ruler where you want the new tab stop positioned. The tab buttons are just to the left of the paragraph symbol at the far right side of the ribbon. From right to left, the buttons are left, center, right, and decimal.

Keep It Together

Formatting changes on tabular data would sure be easier if the data were all one paragraph, wouldn't they? No problem! Press **Shift+Enter** (instead of just **Enter**) at the end of each line as you key in your tabular table. Now any paragraph formatting changes you apply to the tabular data (such as new tab stop placement) affect the entire table, and you don't have to select the entire table first.

Take Me to Your Leader

You may want to create tab stops with *leader* characters. Leaders can be dots, dashes, or a solid line and can only be applied to custom tab stops, not default tab stops. To set leaders for a tab stop, pull down the Format menu and select the Tabs option. In the Tabs dialog box, click on the tab stop where you want to apply the leader in the Tab Stop Position list or type a new setting. Then click next to the type of leader you want to apply in the Leader area of the dialog box. Click on Set and then OK if you are setting more than one tab. Just click on OK for one setting. (By the way, Item 4 under line leaders is good for creating fill-in-the-blank forms!)

Extra! Extra! Read All About Creating Newspaper-Style Columns!

If you're putting together a newsletter or some other type of document that needs multiple columns, Word for Windows' Columns feature makes it easy. These columns are referred to as *snaking columns*, *newspaper-style columns*, or just *text columns*.

The simplest way to turn on columns for the section you're in is the Text Columns button on the toolbar. Just click on the Text Columns button and drag the mouse across to the desired number of columns. You can choose up to six columns. If you need more than six columns, you must use the Columns dialog box, accessible from the Format menu. Multiple text columns are only displayed side-by-side on-screen in Page Layout view or Print Preview.

If you don't want *all* the text in your document to be in columns, you'll need to subdivide your document into multiple sections. In any one section, all

---

What's My Line?

When you format text in multiple columns, having lines separate the columns can often add to the professional look of the document. (In the publishing biz, these lines are known as *rules*.) Word for Windows inserts these rules if you click in the Line Between check box in the Columns dialog box, but you can only see them in Print Preview or when you print the document.

---

the text is either in multiple columns or not. If you want to format some of the text in a document in multiple columns without affecting the text above or below it, select the text, pull down the Format menu, and choose Columns. Specify the number of columns you want in the Number of Columns box. Then, in the Apply To drop-down list, choose Selected Text, and click on OK. Word for Windows inserts section breaks (displayed as double lines) above and below the selected text and formats the text with the number of columns specified.

Common Columnar Catastrophes

The most common column catastrophe is using the space bar to align columns on-screen. Just don't do it. They won't be aligned when you print. Using the wrong tab type can also cause you to tear your hair out. For example, choosing a default left-aligned tab to line up a column of numbers causes your decimal to miss the point.

Word for Windows' text columns feature is great, but not if you can't see your columns side by side. Choose the wrong view and that will be your fate. And, when you finally figure out how to use and view columns, getting the bottom edges even can seem like an impossible task.

As terrific as they are, you may not want your whole document in multiple columns, but how do you turn them off? And create columns of differing widths? You may come to the conclusion that there's absolutely no way. Well, check out the following problems and their solutions, and your columns will start shaping up.

What To Do When Your Columns Turn Reptilian

You've just spent five hours getting the rows and columns for your company's employee phone list to line up just perfectly on your computer screen. Phew! Now, at long last, you're ready to print it. As you eagerly await the pages from your printer, your anticipation turns to horror. Oh no! Nothing's lined up correctly anymore! How can you salvage all your hard work? Don't panic—just read the rest of this chapter.

10 Do's and Don'ts for Avoiding Column Calamities

1. *Do* use custom tab stops to create tabular tables and be sure there is only one tab between each column.

2. *Don't* use spaces to line up columns of text on-screen; use tabs instead.

3. *Do* use decimal-aligned tabs to line up numbers on their decimal points.

4. *Don't* use the Text Column button on the toolbar to turn on columns for selected text. Instead, use the Columns dialog box.

5. *Do* use Page Layout view to display multiple columns on-screen.

6. *Don't* use Page Layout view if you want to maximize your PC's performance. Side-by-side column display consumes quite a bit of your computer's resources.

7. *Do* insert a section break to turn off your columns.

8. *Don't* try to specify different widths for your text columns. You can't. Take a look at Chapter 16 for some other ideas.

9. *Do* use the Keep With Next option in the Paragraph dialog box (accessed from the Format menu) to keep headings in columns with the next paragraph.

10. *Don't* use too many columns on one page. On standard size paper, more than five or six columns makes the text hard to read.

Problem 1:

The columns of your tabular table look fine on-screen but look like snakes on paper

This may be the number-one most common problem people have when switching to Word for Windows (or most other word process- ing programs) from a typewriter. You're using proportional fonts now, pal, and the space bar just doesn't cut it anymore. Never, never, never use the space bar to try to line things up on-screen. They won't be lined up when you print.

Besides, tabs are a whole lot easier to use—especially if you need to change the amount of space between the columns later. Can you imagine adding an extra 12 spaces between two columns on each of 75 rows? No way! If you use tabs and you need to change the dis- tance between two columns, just drag the marker for the tab stop to a different position on the ruler. Pretty slick, eh?

Now you know what to do for future tabular tables, but what can you do about the mess you've gotten yourself into for this one? Well, you need to remove all the spaces between the columns and then replace them with tabs. Probably the easiest way is to select the spaces and then press the **Delete** key. Make sure your spaces are visible (click on the paragraph symbol on the ribbon if they aren't). Drag your mouse to select all the spaces and then zap them with the **Delete** key. Finally, press the **Tab** key ONCE. If your columns aren't lined up the way you want them, you may need to set or adjust cus- tom tab stops.

Problem 2:

You can't select just one column of a tabular table

Perhaps you want to change the font or some other attribute of the text in *just one column* or part of one column in a tabular table. The problem is, when you try to select the column you want, *all* the columns are selected. The solution is to use the select rectangle method. Position your insertion point at the upper left corner of the rectangular area you want to select. Then, while holding down the **Shift** key, move the I-beam pointer to the lower-right corner of the rectangle and click the right mouse button, and there you go.

Problem 3:

You used tabs, but your numbers *still* won't line up on their decimal points

Well, you didn't use a decimal-aligned tab stop, did you? I thought not. If you just use the default, left-aligned tab stops, your numbers flow from the tab stop to the right. So, if you type 123.00 at that tab stop on one line, and 1234.00 on the next line, your decimal points don't line up.

Fortunately, the fix for this problem is simple. If you set custom tab stops (you should have), the first thing to do is to remove the offending tab stop. First, select the text to be modified. Then point to the custom tab stop with the mouse pointer, press the mouse button, drag the tab stop down off the ruler, and release the mouse button. (If you didn't set custom tab stops, skip this step.)

But now your numbers aren't separated from the previous column at all! Don't worry, click on the decimal tab button on the ribbon. (It's the one just to the left of the paragraph symbol.) Finally, click on the bottom half of the ruler where you want the decimal points of your number to line up. If you need to reposition it (or any other custom tab stop), you can just drag it left or right on the ruler.

Problem 4:

When you try to apply formatting changes to a tabular table (like moving tab stops), it only affects the row your insertion point is in

You pressed **Enter** at the end of each line of your tabular table, didn't you? See, if you press the **Enter** key at the end of each line, each line is treated as a separate paragraph. If you want to format your tabular table as one paragraph (and you do), press **Shift+Enter** instead of the **Enter** key by itself when you finish each line.

To clean up your current mess, select the text containing all those nasty Enters, pull down the **Edit** menu, and select **Replace**. In the Find What text box, type ^**p**. In the Replace With text box, type ^**n**. ^p is the code for the paragraph mark, and ^n is the code for a new line. Choose Replace All and your troubles are over.

Problem 5:
Your text columns don't display side-by-side on-screen

You can only see side-by-side columns on-screen in Page Layout view or in Print Preview. In Normal view, your text appears as one narrow column running down the left side of the page. The advantage of Normal view is that it's faster and at least you'll see the column width accurately. In Outline view, your column width doesn't display accurately.

Problem 6:
You can't remember how to create newspaper-style columns with different widths

This is a trick problem. There's no way to do it. All your text columns must have the same width

You Are the Ruler of Your Column Width

If you want to adjust the width of all your columns quickly and easily, the ruler is the way to go. Click on the bottom half of the ruler to the left of the 0 to display the column markers. They appear as brackets on either side of each column. To change the width of your columns, simply drag the column markers and watch all the columns change.

and the same space between columns. Sorry. There is a way to get around this using the Tables feature. It's not perfect, but it may do what you need. Check out Chapter 16 for more information.

Problem 7:
You can't get the bottoms of your text columns to be even

The solution to this problem is simple if you remember the section concepts as they relate to columns. When you insert a *Continuous Section Break*, Word for Windows evens out the columns. To insert a Continuous Section Break, pull down the Insert menu and choose **Break**. Click next to Continuous in the Section Break area and then click on OK. This procedure works well when you're at the end of your columns or if you want to start a new set of columns.

Problem 8:
The lines between your columns aren't visible

You went to all the trouble of telling Word for Windows to insert those nice vertical lines between your text columns and now you can't see them—even in Page Layout view. Well, lines between columns only show up in Print Preview and in print. Sorry. That's just the way it is.

Problem 9:
Your single-column text above multiple-column text suddenly turns into multiple columns

The double line that represents the section break is important. If it's deleted, the text in what was the section above it takes on the column formatting of what was the section below it. In other words, the two sections have been joined and have the same multiple columns. If you notice that you've deleted the section break mark before you take any other action, you can use the Undo command (from the Edit menu) to reverse the deletion. If it's too late for that, position your insertion point at the end of what was the first section and insert a new section break from the Break dialog box, accessible from the Insert menu.

A Final Word on Columns

It takes practice to become really comfortable with columns in all
their varieties, but once Word for Windows' column logic starts to
make sense to you, your difficulties will disappear. Do a lot of test
printing as you're familiarizing yourself with columns to see how
your changes worked. The main thing you need to remember about
tabular tables is to STAY AWAY FROM THE SPACE BAR! Once again,
don't forget to save your work often so that if you make a horrible
mistake, you can call up the saved version.

What To Do When...

Your Graphics Are Grubby

CHAPTER FOURTEEN

Word for Windows can import graphics and manipulate them in thousands of ways. You can get as graphic as community standards will allow. Of course, adding a graphic to your document often just adds one more source of headaches. If you're having problems with graphics, this is the chapter for you.

Why Use Graphics in Word for Windows Documents?

Adding pictures and other graphic images can transform your documents from drab, lifeless pieces of paper into dazzling instruments of persuasion. For example, if you're writing a newsletter on investments, a picture of a stack of money would certainly grab the reader's attention faster than words alone.

Of course, graphics shouldn't just be decoration; they should have *some* relevance to the surrounding text. A picture of an ice cream cone, for example, probably wouldn't be the best choice for your investment newsletter. Unless, of course, you're trying to get your readers to invest in an ice cream truck.

Painting Versus Drawing

Painting programs like Paintbrush create graphics that are made up of thousands, or even millions of little dots, called *bits*. Graphics that are made up of bits are usually called *bitmapped* graphics. *Drawing* programs like Microsoft Draw, however, create graphics made up of objects that can be manipulated independently. Such graphics are called *object-oriented* or *vector* graphics. Bitmapped graphics are usually better for creating images that require lots of detail and subtle changes of color or gray shading. Vector graphics are easier to edit; they also resize beautifully and take up less disk space than bitmapped graphics.

Where Do You Get the Graphics To Use?

Word for Windows comes with its own set of ready-to-use graphics (called *clip art*), which you can add to your documents. You can also buy sets of clip art on diskettes to add variety to your "art" collection. You can use any of a wide variety of graphics programs to create your own graphics from scratch or to modify your clip art. You already own at least two graphics programs—Windows comes with a *painting program* called Paintbrush, and Word for Windows includes its own drawing program called Microsoft Draw.

Other Graphics Programs

If your graphic needs become more sophisticated than Word for Windows alone—or even the graphics programs that come with Word for Windows and Windows—c an handle, consider buying a full-featured graphics program. Programs such as Harvard Graphics for Windows, Microsoft PowerPoint, or CorelDRAW! may meet your needs. These and many other graphics programs offer capabilities far beyond those available to you with just Word for Windows and Paintbrush.

Before you plunk down your money, though, carefully consider *why* you need another graphics program. Some programs can be so ex-cruciatingly difficult to use, they might make you long for the good old typewriter days. If possible, try before you buy. Many vendors let you return a program for a refund within 30 days if it doesn't meet your requirements.

One more thing about other graphics programs. Don't overlook the graphics capabilities of the other non-graphics programs you already own. A spreadsheet program, for example, won't have the power of a full-featured graphics program, but it may include just the feature you're looking for.

Putting Graphics on the Silver Screen

After your graphic is created, Word for Windows makes it ridiculously easy to get it into your document. Just pull down the Insert menu and choose Picture. Find the picture you want (you may need to look around in several

Graphics Can Be Seen Clearly through Windows

One of the best features of Windows is that it insists that every Windows program is compatible in a variety of ways with every other Windows program. So graphics created in any Windows program can be cut or copied to the Windows Clipboard and then pasted into Word for Windows. Of course, the reverse is also true.

directories to find the one that contains your graphic file) and double-click on it. Word for Windows is so clever that it recognizes graphics that were created in other programs and converts them to the proper format for Word for Windows. That's it! When Word for Windows retrieves the graphic, you can size it and crop it to your heart's content.

Why Graphics Sometimes Look Bad

If certain kinds of graphics (bitmapped) aren't sized properly, they can end up looking horribly deformed, if they print at all! If Word for Windows isn't set up right with the correct filters and a printer selected, or if you're in the wrong view, they won't show up at all.

Once you get the graphics on-screen, you'll want to move them to just the right place in the document. But, unless they are framed, they're not going anywhere. Even with a frame, they aren't moving unless you're in the right view. When it comes to resizing your graphics, if you aren't careful, the proportions can get all messed up. You can turn a perfectly good circle into an ugly oval.

Graphic Texts

Once you get a taste of the awesome graphics capabilities of Word for Windows, I *know* you'll want to learn as much as you can about all the available options and applications. Check out Que's *Using Word for Windows 2,* Special Edition, for more information about graphics. Don't miss the section of that book devoted to desktop publishing.

Graphics created in other programs can create special problems. You needed more problems, didn't you? If you don't follow the proper steps, a graphic that should be updated will end up being outdated. I'll show you how to squash these graphic gremlins and others in the following problems and solutions.

10 Do's and Don'ts for Working with Graphics

1. *Do* make sure you have a printer installed and selected in Word for Windows. Without a printer selected, Word for Windows doesn't let you put any graphics in your document.

2. *Don't* use Draft mode when working with graphics. You won't be able to see them.

3. *Do* use the highest video resolution that your system can handle and is comfortable for you. You get a more accurate view of your graphics at higher resolutions.

4. *Don't* expect to see your graphics printed with all their pretty colors unless you have a color printer.

5. *Do* use Page Layout view to see where your graphic is placed on the document.

6. *Don't* use the Link to File option to keep the file size down. It won't. The picture is still part of the document.

7. *Do* use the mouse to make large adjustments to the sizing and cropping of the graphic. Use the Picture dialog box (accessed from the Format menu) to make fine adjustments.

8. *Don't* size graphics with the top, bottom, or side handles. Use the corner handles to ensure that you retain the correct proportions.

9. *Do* frame your pictures so that you can position them at will and text will wrap around them.

10. *Don't* use irrelevant graphics. They just distract from the real message of your document.

Fixing Graphics Problems

Gosh, after reading the beginning of this chapter, it sounds as though graphics are no trouble at all. What could possibly go wrong?

Glad you asked! For graphics to work properly in Word for Windows, your PC needs to be set up properly. Printer problems can put a halt to smooth graphics operations, and there are a few other pitfalls you need to watch out for. I don't want to get too graphic here, so read on.

Problem 1:
All you see on your screen are dumb-looking boxes instead of graphics

You followed all the correct steps to bring a picture into your document, but there's no picture, just a box where the graphic should be. This isn't really a problem at all. You're just in the wrong view mode, or you've chosen to view graphics this way in the Options dialog box.

Word for Windows doesn't display your graphics on-screen in Draft mode. Pull down the View menu and click on Draft to toggle this mode off. If Draft mode isn't on (it doesn't have a check mark next to it), pull down the Tools menu and choose Options. In the Options dialog box, select the View category. Picture Placeholders in the Show Text With section of the dialog box is probably checked. Click on its check box to turn off the option. When you close the dialog box, your graphics appear.

The Picture Placeholders option can be useful if you have a slower system or a very long document with lots of graphics. Displaying graphics takes a lot of computing power and can really slow down your system, so displaying just the placeholders can greatly improve performance. Of course, you can simply use Draft mode, but then you can't see font attributes or accurate line breaks either.

Problem 2:
You can't see graphics or even placeholders on-screen

Oh my! This *does* sound serious. Chances are you have an incorrect or outdated video driver. Try installing your video driver again (hopefully the latest version) from the original Windows diskettes. If this suggestion doesn't solve the problem, call in the genius with the pocket protector. Thank goodness for computer nerds! (I use the term affectionately because, of course, I am one.)

Problem 3:
Word for Windows doesn't let you insert a picture

This problem usually means that you don't have a printer installed or selected in Word for Windows. With no printer selected, Word for Windows simply refuses to let you put a picture in your document. Install and select a printer to solve your problem.

Problem 4:
You want to insert one of Word for Windows' clip art pictures, but you can't remember what they look like from the file names

You've chosen Picture from the Insert menu and have the Picture dialog box staring at you with a list of graphics with cryptic file names. To see what a picture looks like before you insert it into your document, click once on the file name you want to look at and click on the Preview button. The picture appears in the Preview Picture area. Neat!

Problem 5:
Your pictures look weird when you resize them

After you've carefully sized your pictures to get them just right, the last thing you need is to have the pictures look weird. Resizing can cause two kinds of weirdness. First, you might find that you've changed the proportions of your picture and distorted the image. Circles that become ovals or normal sedans that become stretch limousines are dead giveaways.

The solution is to pull down the Format menu, choose Picture, and click on the Reset button in the dialog box to return the picture to its original dimensions. To resize the picture and retain the correct proportions, use only the corner sizing handles, not the ones on the sides, top, or bottom.

The other problem resizing can cause is poor-quality printing or strange banding effects. This problem almost always happens when you resize a bitmapped graphic (not the kind that come with Word for Windows). Bitmapped graphics aren't designed to be resized, even though you can resize them. The only solution is to experiment with different sizes and proportions until you achieve a satisfactory result.

Problem 6:
After resizing a picture, it won't print

Things were going just fine. Your printouts looked great. Then you resized a graphic and it won't print. This usually happens because you are trying to resize a bitmapped graphic. Bitmapped graphics, being just a whole bunch of dots, don't take kindly to resizing. The most effective cure is to resize the picture in the program it was created in and then leave it at 100% in Word for Windows. Delete the picture you have in your current document and insert it again after making the modifications in the picture's native program.

Problem 7:
After inserting a picture, you can't position it

The only graphic item you can position is a *frame*. If you insert a picture into your document without a frame, it's pretty much stuck at the left margin. The solution it to frame it. Select the picture, pull down the Insert menu, and choose **Frame**.

If you're not in Page Layout view, Word for Windows displays a dialog box asking whether you want to be in Page Layout view. You do. Even with a frame around the picture, you can only move a picture in Page Layout view. That's it!

You can position the picture by dragging it or using the Frame dialog box (accessed from the Format menu).

Problem 8:
You need to crop a picture so you see only a portion of it

You have a picture of two people standing in front of a map (Word for Windows comes with just such a picture), and you want to crop it so only one person remains visible. No problem. Position your pointer over one of the handles and hold down the **Shift** key while dragging the mouse to reduce the size of the picture. You aren't actually reducing its size; you're eliminating that portion of the picture. You can also use this cropping method to add "white space" to the picture by expanding the picture while holding down the **Shift** key.

Problem 9:
You can't import a graphic created in another program

You told Word for Windows to insert a picture and selected a file that was created in some other graphics program, and a dialog box appeared, prompting you to specify what type of file it is. Word for

Windows obviously has no clue as to what this file is, or the file would have been converted automatically.

Hijacking Your Files

If you do a lot of importing and exporting of files, especially using unusual formats, consider investing in a good file conversion program. One of the best is Hijack for Windows by Inset Systems. It can deal with just about every file format in existence. If Hijack can't deal with it, it's time to stop using that file format.

There are two possible problems here. This could be a file type that Word for Windows simply doesn't know how to convert. Word for Windows can convert the most popular file types, but not everything. Check the documentation for information on what types of files Word for Windows can convert. One possible solution is go back to the program in which the file was created and see whether it can *export* the file to a format Word for Windows can understand.

Another possibility is that Word for Windows doesn't have the correct *import filter* installed in the WIN.INI file. If you don't care to delve that deeply into Word for Windows' guts, call in the PC pro while you take a coffee break.

Problem 10:
You've inserted some pictures in your document that are linked to the file, but they don't update when you modify the graphic

Word for Windows has a great feature called *link to file*, which allows you to create a link between the document and the graphic file, which was created in another program, on the disk. To use it, just click in the box next to Link to File in the Picture dialog box when you're inserting a picture.

To have Word for Windows update the picture if you've made changes to it in another program, issue specific instructions to do so. Pull down the Edit menu and choose Links. Select the link you want to update and click on the Update Now button. If you want the link updated automatically whenever the graphic file is modified, click in Automatic next to Update.

Problem 11:
You need to modify an inserted picture in Microsoft Draw

You've inserted one of Word for Windows' clip art pictures and you need to modify it. To quickly get the picture into Microsoft Draw, just point to the picture and double-click on it. Word for Windows starts Microsoft Draw with the picture already loaded! Make your modifications, and when you close Draw, a dialog box asking whether you want to update the document appears. Click on Yes to put your revised picture in your document.

Problem 12:
When you print a document, only part of the pictures print

This problem is usually caused by a lack of printer memory. Laser printers are known as *page printers,* which means they need enough internal memory to store the *whole* page they are about to print. Most laser printers don't come standard with enough memory to print a page containing a very large graphic at its highest resolution (usually 300 dots per inch).

The immediate solution is to lower the printer resolution. Choose Print Setup from the File menu and click on Setup. If the resolution is set to 300 dots per inch, try changing it to 150 dots per inch. If that doesn't work, try 75 dots per inch.

Of course, your pictures don't look as good at these lower resolutions, so the ultimate solution, if you're willing to spend a few dollars, is to add memory to your printer. You can add one or two extra megabytes (more than enough) to most laser printers for under $200.

A Final Word on Graphics

Don't be intimidated by Word for Windows' graphic capabilities. With some practice, you'll be knocking out great-looking documents in no time. Please remember to use some restraint when inserting graphics. Like fonts, they can easily be overdone. Pay attention to good-looking, professionally created documents, such as newsletters and magazines, and implement the good ideas you see.

As always, don't forget to save your work regularly. In fact, as you make changes to complex documents containing graphics, it's a good idea to save various versions of them with different file names. Don't be afraid to experiment. Go on—get graphic!

Your Merge Is Mangled

CHAPTER FIFTEEN

You've had merge problems from the minute you got out of bed this morning. You couldn't seem to merge the toothpaste with your toothbrush. In an equally unsuccessful merge attempt, your cream just wouldn't merge with your coffee. (Of course, it merged with the floor just fine!) Driving to work, none of the other drivers on the road would let you merge with traffic. And, now that you finally made it to the office, you just want to produce an uneventful print merge so you can send off those form-letters to your customers announcing the special sale price on blenders.

What Merging Can Do for You

Print Merge is one of Word for Windows' most powerful features. If you're using Word for Windows in a business setting, you need to know about this feature. When you merge, you're combining two files, a *data file* and a *main document*.

The data file contains all the data, or *variable* information, such as customer names and addresses. The main document contains the *static* information. If you're sending a letter to all your customers to announce a new sale, most of the information is duplicated in every letter. The only information that needs to change is the customer name and address information, which is brought in from the data file.

The Print Merge feature is an incredible time saver for creating this sort of *form letter*, as well as for creating mailing labels and envelopes. Some of the terminology and a few of the steps may seem a bit confusing, but it's worth the effort! You may have heard how difficult it is to produce merged documents in other programs—forget about it! If you take some time to explore the possibilities, you'll be merging away like you were born to do it.

Some Basic Print Merge Terminology

The data file that contains all the customer (variable) information is made up of *records* which contain *fields*. In the example, think of a record as a page that contains all the information about a single customer. On the page are places to enter specific items of information that are required for each customer, such as name, address, phone number, etc.

How To Be Outstanding in Your Field

Although fields are one of the primary components in merges, Word for Windows also uses fields in normal, non-merge type documents. You can, for example, insert a Date field in a document to have Word for Windows display the current date. The date is updated whenever you print the document or press **F9** while the insertion point is in the field. You can use fields to prompt for variable information to be entered manually, either during a merge or as a fill-in-the-blanks document.

These items are referred to as fields. In this example, there is a name field, an address field, and a phone number field.

Merging with Word for Windows

You *can* create data files and main documents for your merge manually, but why go to all that trouble when Word for Windows can take you by the hand and gently lead you through the process? To let Word for Windows do all the work, from a blank document, pull down the **File** menu and choose Print **Merge**. A dialog box with a cute diagram showing two documents being funneled into one appears. The first thing you need to do is attach a data file, so click on the Attach Data File button.

The Attach Data File dialog box looks similar to the Open dialog box. If you have a previously created data file, you can choose it from the file name list. To create a new data file, click on the Create Data File button. The Create Data File dialog box is where you assign field names for your data file. Just enter a name of no more than 20 characters with no spaces (such as Fname for the first name field) and click on Add or press **Enter**.

Continue entering fields until you have all the fields you need and then click on OK. Save the data file with a normal file name and, when you close the Save As dialog box by choosing OK, your field names appear as the header row of a *table*. Each column in the table represents a field and each row represents a record. Tables are convenient devices for arranging and manipulating data in rows and columns. Chapter 16 has more information about tables.

Taking a Header

The only other available option (besides Cancel) is the Attach Header File button. When you create a data file, the field names make up the first row (or *header* row). Sometimes you may require a separate header file instead of having the header row attached to the data. One such case is when you import records from another source, such as a database program.

How Many Fields?

To figure out how many fields you need, consider how the data will be used in the main document, not just in the main document you're about to create, but in future main documents too. After all, you can use this data file in a variety of ways. You need a separate field for each type of information you'll need to use independently. For example, if you want to create form letters that refer to your customers by their first names in a future main document, you need to separate first-name and last-name fields.

To enter the data in your data file, just start typing and press **Tab** to move from field to field. If the data you enter in the field doesn't fit on one line, Word for Windows will automatically wrap it on as many lines as necessary. If you want to intentionally enter multiple lines, such as for an address, press **Enter** after each line and then press **Tab** to end the field.

When you reach the end of a row (which is the end of a record), press **Tab** once more, and Word for Windows adds a new row so you're ready to add another record. If you accidentally pressed **Enter** while entering data in the table, press **Backspace** to remove the extra line.

After you enter your data into the data file, close and save it, and you're ready to create your main document. Start typing your form letter in the blank document, using the Insert Merge Field button to insert fields in the main document where you want the data from those fields placed. When you're ready to send the merged documents to the printer, click on the button above the ruler with the picture of two pieces of paper with an arrow pointing to a printer.

Why Merges Misfire

Lack of planning is the most common merge problem. If you don't have all the fields you need for your main document, you won't be able to perform the merge the way you want. Adding punctuation in your data file is also a likely cause of merge formatting problems.

Trying to merge huge data files can put your computer's memory (and your patience) to the test. And speaking of tests, remember Murphy's Law. If you don't do a test print of a few records first, your merge printouts will (almost) always be messed up.

If You Have an Urge To Merge

You can do simple print merges without too much difficulty if you just acquire a basic understanding of the merge concepts. Merge is such a powerful tool, however, you may want to explore it in greater depth than this book can address. *Using Word for Windows 2,* Special Edition has excellent and detailed sections on fields and merging.

When you finally get the labels for your mass mail-merge to print, you'll feel out of sorts if they aren't sorted in zip code order. Along the same lines, you don't always want to merge with all the records in your data file, but how the heck do you select just the records you want? If your merge isn't running on all cylinders, the following problems and their solutions will get you revved up.

Fixing Mishandled Merges

You've finally finished entering the last of your data in your data file. You've created the perfect main document and you're ready to execute the merge. You sit back in your chair watching your printer spit out page after page of perfect form letters. Wait a minute! What's this? Blank lines between the name and address on some of the letters. Is there any way to fix this? Of course there is. Go buy another case of paper and read the following merge tips.

Problem 1:
Your merged documents have blank lines

There are a couple of possible causes for this merge malady. You may have the wrong option selected for the treatment of blank lines, or you may have used the new line command to create new lines in the main document.

To fix the first problem, when you have your main document on-screen and are ready to print, don't click on the little pages-to-printer button. Instead, double-click on the data file name to the right of that button to bring up the Print Merge Setup dialog box and click on the Merge button.

10 Do's and Don'ts for Merry Merging

1. *Do* plan carefully before creating a data file so you'll have all the individual fields you need.

2. *Don't* use spaces or punctuation in your field names. Use an underscore if you need to separate two parts of a field name.

3. *Do* use a separate header file if you're bringing your data in from another program.

4. *Don't* add any spaces or punctuation when entering data in a data file. Add spaces and punctuation in the main document. That way, you won't have any limitations on how you can use the data in the future.

5. *Do* be sure you include all the required fields in your main document.

6. *Don't* use the new line command (**Shift+Enter**) to move to the next line in the main document. Word for Windows can't suppress blank lines if they end with the new line command.

7. *Do* allow Word for Windows to help you set up your data files and main documents. Building these documents manually is more difficult and more likely to result in errors.

8. *Don't* use any punctuation, such as commas, slashes, etc. if you manually create a data file. If you need to add one of these punctuation marks, surround the text containing them with quotes.

9. *Do* a test print with just a couple of records before sending a massive merge to the printer. If there is a problem, you can resolve it without any further deforestation.

10. *Don't* worry about the order of your data file records. If you need to sort them, Word for Windows can handle it within the data file.

In the Treatment of Blank Lines Caused by Empty Fields section, be sure the Skip Completely (As in Form Letter Addresses) option is selected. Also, check your main document to make sure you pressed the **Enter** key at the end of each inserted field instead of the new line command (**Shift+Enter**). If you have any new line commands, delete them and press the **Enter** key. And say good-bye to those blank lines.

Problem 2:
When creating form letters, you can't address some people by first name and others by last name

This is one of the most common merge problems. You created a first-name field and a last-name field and that seemed perfectly adequate at the time. But you don't want to address everyone by first name, and you *can't* use just the last name. If you type **Dear Mr.** followed by a last name code, Sally Smith might be a little upset, or at least she'll know this wasn't a personally prepared letter.

The solution to this problem is a salutation field. A salutation field gives you the opportunity to enter how each person in your data file should be addressed. Depending on how well you know Sally Smith, you might enter **Sally**, **Ms. Smith**, or **My Pal Sal** in the salutation field.

Problem 3:
You can't remember how to create mailing labels

If you don't create a lot of mailing labels, this procedure is easy to forget. Fortunately, Word for Windows makes creating mailing labels so easy, it won't take much to jog your memory. Pull down the File menu and choose New. You usually create documents based on the Normal template, but in this case, you use the MAILLABL template by double-clicking on MAILLABL in the Use Template list. (In the New section, leave Document selected.) Choose the correct type of printer in the Mailing Labels dialog box (Laser or Dot Matrix) and then select the kind of mailing labels you have.

When you select your labels, Word for Windows goes through a few gyrations getting representations of labels on-screen and then asks whether you want to print a single label or multiple labels. If you're merging with a data file, you want multiple labels. Then Word for Windows asks a trick question, `Are the merge names and data contained in two separate files, a header file and a data file?`

If the Label Fits . . .

When you use the MAILLABL template, Word for Windows presents you with a selection of labels from which to choose, but they're all Avery labels. Avery labels are an industry standard and are available virtually everywhere. Your life will be a lot easier if you just go with the program and get Avery labels so you can use one of the label definitions on the list. If you *must* buy something else, be sure you know which Avery label it's compatible with. One more thing, if you have a laser printer, buy high-quality labels designed for laser printers. It's not worth messing up your expensive laser printer just to save a few bucks.

If the data is in a table with field names as the first row, the answer to this question is No. (You'd answer Yes if you were merging with a data file from another program.) Attach the data file by selecting it in the Attach Data File dialog box. Now you need to add the fields to the label.

The trick here is to use the special characters to add spaces or punctuation. For example, if you have an Fname and an Lname field, you'd want both these fields on the same line separated by a space. Double-click on Fname in the Field Names list and then double-click on space in the Special Characters list. Finally, double-click on Lname.

Continue adding fields until you have all your name and address information (or whatever) structured the way you want it in the Sample Mailing Label section, and then click on Done. There's one trap to avoid here. Don't use the new line option in the Special Characters list because Word for Windows can't suppress blank lines if you do. Use the new paragraph option to move to the next line.

Word for Windows fills in all the labels with field codes that match the structure you specified. Click OK to clear the dialog box that tells you the main document has been set up. All that's left to do is to load the labels in the printer and click the merge to printer button.

Problem 4:
You need to select certain records to merge with

With the main document on-screen, double-click on the data file name above the ruler on the right side. Next, click on Merge. In the Print Merge dialog box, click on Record Selection. The Record Selection dialog box allows you to specify criteria for any of the fields.

For example, if you want to send letters only to your Pennsylvania customers, click on State in the Field Name list, then click on Equal to (the default) in the Is list, type PA in the Compared To text box, click on Add Rule, and then click on OK. You can add more rules to narrow or widen the selection criteria. Now when you complete the merge, only those records that meet the criteria are merged.

Problem 5:
You receive an error message when you try to merge to a document instead of the printer

Sometimes you want to merge to a document instead of the printer so you can see what your documents look like (and make adjustments if necessary) before printing them. To do this, click the icon above the ruler with two pages pointing to one page. But if you're low on memory or disk space, there may not be enough room to merge to a document. The solution is to free up some memory by erasing some files from your hard disk or closing some documents or other applications. Of course, you can always just merge to the printer.

Problem 6:

You want to use a different font on some of the merged data

You're creating a form letter and you want the recipient's first and last name to stand out. Setting them in a different and perhaps larger font would do it. But how? You could merge to a document and then edit the data on every page, but there's no need. The easy way to do this is to apply the new formatting (fonts, point size, and whatever else you want) to the field code in the main document. When you merge the file, the formatting carries over.

Problem 7:

You can't tell whether all the records were merged because they aren't in order

After printing several hundred form letters, you want to be able to go through them and make sure your best customers are included. But because they aren't in alphabetical order, you have to go through almost the entire stack of pages to find the ones you're looking for. Not only that, but when you print labels to do your mailings, you're losing money because they aren't sorted in zip code order. Word for Windows' Sort feature is the solution to both these problems.

The Keys to Success

Sort keys are simply the basis for the sort. If you think of the white pages of a phone book as a sorted data file, sort key 1 is the last name and sort key 2 is the first name. The names are alphabetized by last name, but if there is a tie (two identical last names, such as Miller), the second sort key comes into play and breaks the tie, placing Albert Miller before Michael Miller. You can use the third sort key to break a two-way tie.

With the data file on-screen, click on the S button on the toolbar to access the Sort Records dialog box. Now, simply click on the fields you want for your first, second, and third sort keys, choose ascending or descending for each key, and click on OK. Zap! The records are sorted. You might want to sort them one way (alphabetically by last and then first name) for the letters you're printing and another (by zip code) for mailing labels.

A Final Word on Merging

The whole point of word processing is to eliminate as much repetitive work as possible. And what could be more repetitive than typing the same letter over and over with only the recipient's name and address being changed for each one? When you have this kind of repetitive task to perform, try to think of the ways Word for Windows can save you time. If you do, you'll use the Print Merge feature all the time.

Keep in mind that you can use your data files with as many main documents as you like. If you have several data files with the same fields, you can use one main document with multiple data files. As Mergin' Mike says, "Every hour invested in exploring the merge features saves you many."

What To Do When. . .

Your Tables Aren't Set Right

CHAPTER SIXTEEN

Using the Tables feature to organize your information into rows and columns can make the task so easy, you'll wonder how you ever got along without this amazing tool. Working effortlessly in a table can be exhilarating. However, trying to maneuver in a table that isn't set right can be an exercise in sheer terror. If you've been having nightmares about your table settings, this chapter is just for you.

Table Talk

Word for Windows provides the Tables feature as a tool for organizing information into rows and columns. But isn't a table kind of like a column (discussed way back in Chapter 13)? Congratulations—you've been paying attention! Although tables and columns do similar jobs, each is better for different types of things.

The Difference between Tables and Columns

Tables let you work in a visible grid made up of rows and columns. The rectangular box that is the intersection of a row and a column is called a *cell*. Cells are where you enter and edit all your table data. You'll find that editing, sorting, swapping columns, adding printing borders, and even calculating numbers in tables is a snap—once you learn some table manners.

You can also use Tables as an *alternative* to Word for Windows' text columns feature.

> **Message for Merge Maniacs**
>
> The last chapter revealed that the normal structure for a data file is a table. Although you don't need to know much about tables to work with these data files, a good understanding of tables helps you to work more effectively and make your merging maximally manageable.

Why would you want to do that? Remember that Word for Windows only lets you have equal-width text columns. If you want to create multiple columns with different widths, Tables makes it possible. The downside is that one cell of a table can't be split between two pages. Therefore, you have to create a separate, one-row table for each page you want to create. Boy! That could sure be a pain to format and edit. Oh well, nothing's perfect.

Building the Perfect Table

When you create a table, you tell Word for Windows how many rows and columns you want. Keep in mind that you can always add or delete rows or columns as needed. The easiest and most visual way to start a table is with the Table button on the toolbar.

After you click on the Table button, a grid appears on-screen. You click on the grid and drag the mouse down and to the right for as many rows and columns as you need. If you need more rows and columns than the grid initially displays, keep dragging and the grid expands.

The number of rows and columns is displayed at the bottom of the grid as you drag the mouse. If, for example, you see 7 x 8 Table at the bottom of the grid just before you release the mouse button, you wind up with a 7-row-by-8-column table.

Enter and format data in cells just the way you would in a normal document. If you enter more text than fits in a cell, Word for Win-dows automatically wraps the text and expands the cell to make room for the next line. You can move to a cell by clicking on it or using **Tab** and **Shift+Tab**. You can also

> **Table Talk—the Book**
>
> Tables are one of the more powerful and useful tools in Word for Windows. If you want to fully exploit their power, Que's *Using Word for Windows 2,* Special Edition tells you everything you need to know.

use the arrow keys for navigation, but, if the cells contain data, arrow navigation is cumbersome because the insertion point has to move over each character before moving to the next cell.

By default, the ruler displays the *table scale* when your insertion point is in a table. You can cycle through the other two ruler scales (tab and margin) by clicking on the symbol that is just to the left of 0. While in the table scale, you can use the T marks on the ruler to alter column or cell widths. When you reach the end of a page and find yourself going to the next one, press the **Tab** key.

Why Some Tables Are Shaky

Isn't it frustrating that, now that you know how to set decimal tab stops, the darn Tab key doesn't seem to work correctly in tables? Getting numbers to line up on their decimal points in tables can seem like the impossible dream. What if you want to add some normal text above the table at the top of your document? There must be a way to position the insertion point above the table.

After you finally get your cells adjusted and text aligned, printing can become a real problem. How can you print that table with one cell that spans more than one page? Trying to sort the data in a table by more than one sort criterion can make you feel like you're really on shaky ground with tables. You'll find the answers to these and other deep dark table mysteries in the remainder of the chapter.

Fixing Bad Tables

You've decided to use the Tables feature to create a two-column format with different-width columns. You create a one-row by two-column table and then start typing your first column. Naturally, you forget that your text won't snake to the next column. When you realize you've messed up, you try to print your document. Everything past the bottom of page one is gone! Can there be a happy ending to this story? Well, let's just table the issue for now while you read the rest of the chapter.

Problem 1:
You can't select part of the text from two cells

You want to underline just the last few words in one cell and the first few in the next. But every time you try to select just that specific text, the entire contents of both cells are selected.

10 Do's and Don'ts for Tip-Top Tables

1. *Do* use the Column Width dialog box to precisely adjust the width of columns and individual cells.

2. *Don't* type more than a page of text in one cell. A cell can't span pages.

3. *Do* use the Borders feature to add printable gridlines. The gridlines you see on-screen don't show up on your printouts.

4. *Don't* press **Enter** to move to the next cell—it doesn't work. Press **Tab** instead.

5. *Do* determine and set your left and right margins prior to creating your table. Changing them after a table exists can have disastrous results.

6. *Don't* keep pressing **Tab** to get out of a table. You'll just add more rows. Use the down arrow key or **Ctrl+End** to get to the bottom of the document and past the last table.

7. *Do* select an individual cell to adjust the width of that one cell.

8. *Don't* turn off nonprinting characters when working in a table. You need to see the end-of-cell and end-of-row marks while working in tables.

9. *Do* perform multiple sorts to simulate a multi-key sort in a table.

10. *Don't* forget that the fork goes on the left and the spoon goes on the right when you set a table.

Unfortunately, you can't select a portion of two cells. As soon as you cross a cell's boundary while selecting, you're selecting entire cells. The solution to this problem is to make the changes in one cell and then make changes in the next.

Problem 2:
Those nifty table gridlines don't show up when you print

Sad but true, the gridlines don't print. But you can use the Border feature to add the gridlines to your table! Select the portion of the table for which you want gridlines. (You can select the entire table choosing Select Table from the Table menu.)

Pull down the Format menu and choose Border. In the Preset section of the Border Cells dialog box, click on Grid and click OK. You can also choose a different line style for the outline of the table in the Line section of the dialog box if you like. After closing the dialog box, click anywhere inside (or outside) the table so that you can see the lines you applied.

Problem 3:
You can't adjust the width of a single cell

If you try adjusting the width of a single cell by dragging its edge, the width of the entire column changes. In order to change just a single cell, you first must select that cell. That's it!

Problem 4:
You can't get your numbers to line up on their decimal points

This is one of the more common complaints people have while working in tables. The solution is to use a decimal tab. First, select

the cells that contain (or will contain) the numbers you need deci-
mally aligned. Now, toggle the ruler scale from the table scale to the
tab scale by clicking on the symbol to the left of the 0 on the ruler
until the little upside-down T marks are visible.

Click on the Decimal Tab button (the one with an arrow and a dot)
on the ribbon and then place your tab by clicking where you want it
on the bottom half of the ruler. Zap! All the numbers are lined up
properly. Pretty slick, eh?

Problem 5:
You've typed more than a page of text in one cell and now it won't print

The problem isn't *too* difficult to fix. You have two choices. You can
either convert the table to normal text or you can add extra rows to
the table and cut and paste some of the text into the new rows.

Frankly, if you have that much text in one cell, it probably doesn't
belong in a table in the first place. To convert the table to text, select
the *contents* of the entire table, pull down the Table menu, and select Convert Table to Text. In the Convert Table to Text dialog box,
you have three choices for how the text will be converted. The cells
can be separated with paragraph marks, tabs (the default), or commas. With your long cell entry, probably the best choice is paragraph
marks. Click on your choice and then on OK.

To insert new rows, select one or more rows of the table by clicking
in the selection bar to the left of one of the rows, pulling down the
Table menu, and choosing Insert Rows. When the new rows appear,
select some of the text from the long cell, cut it, and, after positioning the insertion point in another cell, choose Paste from the Edit
menu. Oh, and don't let this happen again.

Problem 6:

You created a table at the top of your document and now you can't position your insertion point above the table to type normal text

After inserting a table, you may decide that you need to type a title and perhaps a paragraph of text above the table. No problem. Simply position the insertion point in any cell in the top row of the table and press **Ctrl+Shift+Enter**.

Problem 7:

You can't sort your table data using more than one criterion

Your table consists of first names in one column, last names in the next, and addresses in the third. You want to sort the rows so that the data is in alphabetical order primarily by last name and secondarily by first name. (Check out Chapter 15 for a more detailed discussion of sort keys.)

Let's Split This Crazy Scene

If you need to type some normal text in the middle of a table, you must split the table. Just position the insertion point in any cell of the row *below* the place you want to enter text and press **Ctrl+Shift+Enter**. If you want to join the two segments of the table back together, position the insertion point to the left of the paragraph mark and tap **Delete**.

The problem is, unless you're using a data file, Word for Windows can only sort on one key.

If you only sort on the first name, you could end up with Tom Smith, followed by Bill Smith, followed by Gail Smith. Is there a way around this unconscionable Word for Windows limitation?

You betcha! Just do several sorts. Position your insertion point anywhere in the table, pull down the Tools menu, and choose Sorting. In the Sorting dialog box, specify ascending (A to Z) or descending (Z to A) and then the field number for the sort. The field number is the column on which you want to base the sort. If the first names are in column 1, specify 1 as the field number and click OK. After the data is sorted on the first names, repeat the process, but this time sort on the field containing the last names (probably field 2).

Problem 8:
You need to calculate numbers in your table

It would sure be great if Word for Windows could add up numbers for you because your pocket calculator needs new batteries. Well, it can! Select the numbers you want to add, pull down the Tools menu, and choose Calculate. The status bar at the bottom of the screen displays the result of the calculation, and the result is also cop-

> ### Numbers, Numbers, Numbers!
>
> Word for Windows tables are not the easiest tool to use for sophisticated number crunching. If you do a lot of calculating, consider investing in a spreadsheet program. You can even link segments of a Windows spreadsheet to your Word for Windows document. Microsoft makes a very nice spreadsheet program called Excel. (And it just so happens that Que has a book called *Oops! Excel*—just in case!)

ied to the Clipboard. Position the insertion point where you want to place the result of the calculation and choose Paste from the Edit menu.

A Final Word on Tables

Tables can help you produce rows and columns much more easily than any other method in Word for Windows' arsenal. Spend some time getting acquainted with the feature and you'll find it indispens-able. When working with Tables, many of the editing changes you make have the potential to wreak havoc with your entire document, so remember to save your work regularly. You'll be glad you did.

What To Do When...

Your Macros Malfunction

CHAPTER SEVENTEEN

In previous chapters, I may mention that one feature or another is one of Word for Windows' most powerful, flexible, or useful features. Well, this chapter is about the *most powerful feature in* Word for Windows. And, because it's the most powerful feature, it's also the most *troublesome* feature.

Macros give you the ultimate power to mold Word for Windows to your requirements. Because macros can save you more time and keystrokes than any other Word for Windows feature, this chapter is perfect for lazy people (like me).

What Macros Are and How They Can Save You Oodles of Time

Word for Windows is a really powerful and easy-to-use word processing program. But even with all this terrific power, performing repetitive tasks can become a real chore. That's where macros come in.

Even simple tasks, if repeated often enough, can take up too much of your time. If one of the things you do regularly is select a paragraph and apply bold and italic to it, for example, you can create a macro that saves you several keystrokes or mouse actions each time you perform this task. As long as you do everything right, macros are great!

Basic Macros?

Although you can create some really useful macros just by recording actions with Word for Windows' macro recorder, you need to do a little computer programming to automate some very complex tasks. For this purpose, Word for Windows includes a macro programming language called *WordBasic*. Programming in WordBasic can get pretty complicated, so I won't try to cover it here. If you want more information on WordBasic, there is extensive documentation in Word for Windows' on-line help system.

We Are the World

If you want *all* your macros created as global macros, pull down the File menu, choose the Template option, and when the dialog box appears, click next to Global in the Store New Macros and Glossaries As section of the dialog box. If you choose With Document Template, macros will just be available when using the current template—unless, of course, the current template is NORMAL.DOT in which case the macro will be global. You could always leave the default choice as Prompt for Each New so you have the option to decide.

How To Record a Macro

Nothing could be easier than recording a simple macro! First, you need to decide where you want the macro to be available. Do you want it available anywhere, in any document? If so, you want to create a *global* macro. If you just want the macro available when you use a specific template, you must let Word for Windows know that.

Keep in mind, however, that if you create a macro for the

NORMAL.DOT template, Word for Windows assumes it's a global macro and makes it available with any document you use. If you're creating a document based on another template, Word for Windows prompts you to find out whether to save the macro as global or just in this template.

After you've made your decision about where the macro will be available, pull down the Tools menu and choose the Record Macro option. Give the macro a name without an extension and select shortcut keys if you like.

If you want to be more descriptive, add some text in the Description box. When you click OK, you start recording the macro. Everything you do from this point—and I mean *everything*—is being recorded. It's best to stick with the keyboard for macros because certain mouse actions can mess up your macros. (You can tell you're recording because the right side of the status bar displays REC.) So carry out the steps required to do what you want to do and then pull down the Tools menu and choose the Stop Recorder option. That's it!

Playing Back a Macro

When you need to use a macro, you can play it back in one of two ways. You can press the shortcut keys you assigned to the macro when you recorded it. Or, you can pull down the Tools menu and choose the Macro option. In the Macro dialog box, scroll through the list of macros until you find the one you want, click on it, and then click the Run button. You can also press **Enter** after clicking on the macro, or just double-click on the macro to start it. You may need to scroll down to see the macro name before you can execute it.

The macro will faithfully reproduce the actions you specified when you recorded it. If all you did while recording the macro was type **HELLO**, when the macro finishes running, you'll see HELLO on-screen.

What Can Muck Up Your Macros

Missing macros make you miserable. You can lose your macros by assigning them to the wrong template or even forgetting their names, which is especially frustrating if you've assigned a shortcut key to the macro. It's easy to forget to save your macros too, but you probably won't let that happen more than a couple of times.

Selecting text while recording a macro can certainly cause its share of problems. If you try to use the mouse to select text while recording, it just won't work. Using the mouse for almost anything while recording can mess up macros.

If you don't record your macro just right, it may not do what you intended. Macros can become fairly complex and end up having a mind of their own. Then, even when a macro is working just fine, there's the temptation to edit them to get rid of any subtle problems. That's when trouble can really start.

How Macros Go Bad

You're creating a macro, selecting text, choosing items from dialog boxes—in general, just macroing up a storm. But when you play the macro back, it doesn't do anything else after the first couple of steps. What happened? Can you ever learn to be a macro wizard? Don't worry, there really aren't too many things that can go wrong with simple recorded macros, and I give you the solutions to those problems here.

10 Do's and Don'ts for Macros

1. *Do* decide where you want your macros to be available—globally or just with the current template.

2. *Don't* use the default macro names. You'll never remember what the macros were designed to do.

3. *Do* use keystrokes for making choices in dialog boxes and selecting text while recording a macro. Many mouse activities are recorded improperly or not at all.

4. *Don't* record a macro to perform a task that already has a keyboard shortcut or a button to access the feature. Just use the keyboard shortcut or click the button.

5. *Do* assign macros to menus to make them more accessible.

6. *Don't* record a macro just to insert text or graphics. You can store these things as glossaries.

7. *Do* pull down the File menu and choose the Save All option to ensure your macro is safe after recording it.

8. *Don't* use macros to apply complex formatting to your document. Styles generally work much better for this purpose.

9. *Do* learn a little WordBasic after you get comfortable with simple recorded macros.

10. *Don't* edit your macros if they're working fine and are fast enough. If it ain't broke, don't fix it.

Problem 1:

The macro won't play *or* You can't find the macro

You've tried everything. You pulled down the Tools menu and chose the Macro option, and the macro wasn't there. You pressed the shortcut key and nothing happened. Where is that darn macro? The probable cause is that you saved the macro with a specific template and not as a global macro. If a macro is saved with a specific template, it's only available when you are creating a document based on that template.

To copy the contents of a template macro to a new, global macro, start a new document based on the template where the errant macro was created. Now pull down the Tools menu, choose the Macro option, and then select the macro you want to copy from the Macro Name list. Click on the Edit button and select the entire macro by pointing in the selection bar area and clicking the left mouse button while pressing **Ctrl**. Pull down the Edit menu and choose Copy to place a copy of the macro on the Clipboard.

Now close the document without saving any changes and then start a new document based on the NORMAL.DOT template. Pull down the Tools menu and select Macro. Enter a name for your macro (it can be the same name you used for the template macro) and click on the Edit button. Select everything on-screen, using the same method you used to select the template macro, and then press the **Delete** key. Finally, pull down the Edit menu and choose the Paste option. There's your macro! Now pull down the File menu and select the Save All option (and answer yes to all the dialog boxes) to save all the changes. You now have a new global macro.

Problem 2:

You can't select text while recording a macro

You're probably trying to use the mouse to select the text, and Word for Windows just beeps at you because you're trying to do something that it doesn't allow. While you're recording a macro, you must use the keyboard to select text—you just can't use the mouse.

Problem 3:

Items you've chosen from dialog boxes during macro recording don't work when the macro is played back

This sounds like another case of using the mouse instead of the keyboard. Play it safe; use the Tab key, space bar, and arrow keys to choose any items from dialog boxes while recording a macro.

Problem 4:

It takes too many keystrokes or mouse actions to play a macro

When is a short macro not a time-saver? When you have to pull down the Tools menu, choose Macro, and then select the macro from the list before you can play it!

The solution is to assign a shortcut key combination to the macro, so you can activate it by pressing those keys. You can assign Ctrl + another key as the shortcut keys or Ctrl+Shift (the default) and another key on the keyboard. Because Word for Windows uses Ctrl plus many other keys for internal Word for Windows functions, it's usually best to use Ctrl+Shift with another key.

To assign a Ctrl+Shift shortcut key, drop down the Key list in the Record Macro dialog box and select a key. If that key combination is already assigned to a macro, you'll see what that assignment is next to Currently at the bottom of the Shortcut Key section of the dialog box. If this is the case, just choose another key.

Problem 5:

It's too hard to remember what shortcut key is assigned to a macro

Shortcut keys are easy to assign, and they make running a macro fast and easy—if you remember which keys were assigned to the macro. If you have memory problems (and I really mean *you*, not your computer system!), consider assigning the macro to a menu. The macro name will then be a menu choice at the bottom of any of the menus you assign it to.

To assign a macro to a menu, pull down the Tools menu, choose Options, press **Ctrl+End**, and then press the **up arrow** twice to select the Menus category. Pull down the menu list to select the menu you want to contain the macro. The menu names have funny ampersands (&) in them, but don't let that throw you. If you just imagine that the ampersands are missing, the menu names are easily recognizable.

Choose a menu that makes sense for the macro you're assigning. If you are assigning a macro that formats text, you might want to choose the Format menu. If the macro involves table manipulation, the Table menu might be a good choice.

After choosing a menu, be sure Macros (instead of Commands) is selected in the Show section of the dialog box. Select the macro you want to assign from the macros list, then click on Add, and then close the dialog box. To play the macro, just pull down the menu where you added the macro and choose it.

Tooling Macros

You can even assign a macro to a toolbar button. Pull down the Tools menu, choose Options, and then choose the Toolbar category. Click on the down arrow to the right of the Tools to Change drop-down list. Click on the button you want to replace with a macro. If you don't want to eliminate any of your current buttons, click on one of the spaces between two buttons to add a new button. Next, scroll up and down the Button list and choose a button with an appropriate icon. Finally, select the macro to assign to the button from the Macros list and click on Change and then Close.

Problem 6:
You can't find your global macro

When you create or modify a global macro, you must tell Word for Windows that you want to save the global glossary and command changes. Word for Windows prompts you to do this when you exit the program, but don't wait until then. Instead, immediately after creating a macro, pull down the File menu and choose the Save All option to save the global glossary and command changes.

Now you can work with greater peace of mind. Oh, but what about that macro you forgot to save earlier? Unfortunately, once you exit Word for Windows without saving the global glossary and command changes, you can't get the macro back. Sorry. Do be more careful next time.

Problem 7:
Your macro doesn't do *exactly* what you intended

You've spent a great deal of time creating a macro, and now, when you run the macro, you discover a typo in the text the macro enters. Fortunately, you don't have to rewrite the entire macro—you can edit the macro and fix those nasty typos.

Pull down the Tools menu, choose the Macro option, select the macro you want to edit, and then click on the Edit button. Now, *carefully* replace the errors with the correct text. You can also replace commands, but, unless you are comfortable with WordBasic, you run the risk of messing up the whole thing.

> ### Don't Fix Those Errors
>
> What sort of stupid advice is this? Let me explain. Often, when you record a macro, you make a mistake and then correct the mistake before stopping the recorder. You might be tempted to edit the macro to fix the mistake. But if the macro is working, even if it performs an extra step along the way, you may want to leave it alone. My advice is that the time required to perform the extra step probably isn't even noticeable, but fixing the macro could mess it up all together.

A Final Word on Macros

No other Word for Windows feature offers as much return on your investment of time as macros. The toughest thing for new users to figure out about macros is when to use them. Keep macros in mind when you do *anything* in Word for Windows. If you need to repeat the task, make it a macro. The more you learn about macros, the better your understanding of Word for Windows in general becomes. Oh, and don't forget to save them!

Your Styles Aren't Stylish

CHAPTER EIGHTEEN

Styles let you maintain a consistent look for all your different types of documents. Sure, you can use a zillion Word for Windows features in each document and then change them as necessary—but why waste time when Word for Windows' Style feature can do all the dirty work? Of course, anything that makes your life this simple is bound to cause you problems at some point, which is why this chapter exists. Read on if you want to be a *stylish* Word for Windows user!

Getting Stylish

A style is a set of character and paragraph formats that is stored to-gether under one name. Styles let you effortlessly make wholesale changes to your document's formatting and ensure that all the elements of a given variety have the same attributes. Not only can you use styles to maintain consistency within documents, but you can also use them to maintain consistency for all documents with the same sorts of elements.

Styles can become even more important when creating complex formats. Your company might want to create a particular *look* for all customer proposals, for example. There might be specifications for several levels of headings, body text, tabular tables, or whatever. By creating styles to cover all these document elements, everyone in the company can effortlessly produce consistent documents that meet the company's standards.

What Makes a Style Stylish

Styles can include just about any of the elements you'd add to your documents manually. Here are some of the things you could have in a style:

- Font changes or other character formatting, such as bold or italic

- Paragraph formatting, such as line spacing and alignment changes

- New tab custom stops

- Frames with varying sizes or positions

- Borders around paragraphs

Applying Some Style

Everything you write in Word for Windows is based on *some* style. The default style is called Normal and includes any formatting you've chosen as your formatting defaults. Word for Windows also includes three other standard styles for headings. You can apply these heading styles, in addition to Normal, to any paragraph in any document.

You can apply a standard style to a paragraph by simply positioning the insertion point anywhere in the paragraph and choosing the style from the drop-down list on the ribbon (just to the left of the Font list).

Which Way Are You Heading?

Word for Windows includes a number of predefined styles which are automatically applied with certain operations. Heading styles, for example, are automatically applied when you create headings in outline view. Footnotes are another example of where Word for Windows automatically applies styles.

Changing Your Style

Styles can easily be modified to meet your changing requirements. To change a style, pull down the Format menu and select Style. Click on the down arrow to the right of the Style Name box to view the list of currently defined styles. Click on the name of the style you want to change and then choose the Define button.

The Style dialog box expands, presenting you with buttons for the various formatting options you might want to change. For example, if you want to include a font change, choose the Character button in the Change Formatting portion of the dialog box and make the desired font change. Choose OK to close the dialog box.

After you've made all your changes, review the Description area of the Style dialog box to be sure it includes everything you want and click on the Change button. If the style you're changing is one of

Word for Windows' predefined styles, you'll need to confirm that you want to change the properties of this standard style. Finally, click on Close. When you exit Word for Windows, answer yes when asked whether you want to save the global glossary and command changes.

Creating Your Own Style

To create a style from scratch, you can pull down the Format menu, choose Style, and then assign a name and whatever characteristics you want through a series of dialog boxes.

Styles Have No Character

A style can't affect just some characters in a paragraph. You can't, for example, apply a style to a single word or phrase within a paragraph because the style is applied to the *entire paragraph*. Remember that.

Although this method is effective, there is an even easier way. Simply create the paragraph with all the attributes you want the style to contain, and then create the new style based on these changes. The paragraph might be a heading or body text or any other whole paragraph element of the document that requires special formatting.

After the paragraph has been entered and formatted, and with the insertion point still in the paragraph, select the name of the current style on the ribbon (usually Normal), and type the new name you want to assign for your new style.

Finally, click anywhere in your document to complete the style creation process. When you save the document, the new styles you created in that document are saved with it. You can also add styles to the template your document is based on, or create styles directly in any of your templates. Adding styles to the current template is most easily accomplished while creating styles through the Style dialog box, accessible through the Format menu.

What Causes Things To Go Out of Style

Like macros in the previous chapter, lost styles are the most common cause of style stalemates. While we're on the subject of getting lost, if you don't know which style is applied to which paragraph, you won't be in style. And when it comes to applying styles, you have to apply yourself properly. Applying a style to just a portion of a paragraph doesn't work.

There's nothing more certain than change, especially when it comes to styles. When you put your styles through changes, you want the changes to be there the next time you use Word for Windows. If you don't follow the proper procedures, they won't be. You also want to be able to change smoothly from one style to the next. If you don't know what you're doing, the next style may take effect before you're ready.

Fixing Style Problems

If things go wrong while you're working with styles, read on and you'll figure out how to fix all your major style problems (except maybe what to do with that Nehru jacket and bell bottom outfit you have left over from high school).

Problem 1:
You can't create a style

If you forgot to enter a new, unique name for your style, you'll probably end up modifying an existing style. Each style must have its own name. Pull down the Format menu and select Style. The text in the Style Name text box is highlighted, so just type in the name for your new style and click Define.

10 Do's and Don'ts for Stellar Styles

1. *Do* use unique names for each style in your document. If you type a duplicate name, you risk altering the original style with that name and messing up your entire document.

2. *Don't* try to end the application of a style by pressing **Enter**; it doesn't work. You must apply a new style to the next paragraph or use the Next Style feature when creating a style through the Style dialog box.

3. *Do* expand the Style Width Area so you can see which style each paragraph is using when you have several different styles in a document.

4. *Don't* try to specify a style for just a portion of a paragraph. Styles are applied to the entire paragraph.

5. *Do* print a list of your document's styles and their attributes to use as a guide in applying them.

6. *Don't* apply a style to a paragraph that is already formatted with similar attributes. You'll get unpredictable results.

7. *Do* create a new template with its own set of styles for each type of document you create to promote consistency when creating future documents of that kind.

8. *Don't* alter the Normal style. If you do, all the other styles based on the Normal style will be altered too.

9. *Do* merge the styles from one document or template to another to share styles between documents.

10. *Don't* forget to save your document if you want to preserve any styles you've created for it. If you close a document without saving, any styles created in that document, but not added to the template during creation, are lost forever.

If you're going to want to save the style with the current template, click in the Add to Template check box at the bottom of the dialog box. Include any formatting attributes by using the buttons in the Change Formatting area of the dialog box. Finally, click on Add, then Close. If the current template is NORMAL.DOT, you'll be prompted to save global glossary and command changes when you exit Word for Windows. Answer yes so the style will always be available.

Problem 2:
You can't apply a style

Applying a style is a simple matter of positioning the insertion point in the paragraph you want the style applied to and selecting it from the ribbon or the Style dialog box. To apply a style from the ribbon, click on the down arrow to the right of the style box on the ribbon (the first one on the left end of the ribbon) and click on the desired style name in the drop-down list. If you want to apply a style to multiple paragraphs, select the paragraphs before applying the style.

A common error is to try to apply a style to just a portion of a paragraph. Styles can affect only entire paragraphs. If you select a word or sentence in a paragraph and try to apply a style to it, the style is applied to the whole paragraph. You'll have to manually apply formatting changes to text that is less than a paragraph.

Problem 3:
You can't modify a style

The most likely reason you can't modify a style is that you can't find it to begin with. Make sure you're using a document based on the template the style was created in. Once you've found the style, the steps to modify it are pretty straightforward.

Pull down the Format menu and select Style. Use the down arrow next to the Style Name box to drop down a list of styles and click on the style you want to change and then click on Define. Use the buttons in the Change Formatting area of the dialog box to make your modifications to the style and then click on Change and then click Close. Just as with adding a new style based on the NORMAL.DOT template, when you exit Word for Windows, you're asked whether you want to save the global glossary and command changes. Answer yes to retain the modifications you made to the style.

Problem 4:
Creating a style by example changes portions of the paragraph

When you create a style by using an existing paragraph, Word for Windows does its best to figure out what you want. If, for example, most of the paragraph contains 18-point type, but a few words are set in 12-point type, Word for Windows does the logical thing and uses the format that covers the majority of the paragraph.

When you complete the style creation process, which applies the new style to the paragraph, the little bit of text that was formatted in 12-point type takes on the overall style's text attributes and becomes 18-point type. If you still want that text to be in 12-point type, you must select it and apply the appropriate point size. In the future, create a style before you enter any text that doesn't conform to the attributes you want in the style.

Problem 5:
You created several styles while working in one document, and they're not available in a second document

If you want to create styles that are available for other documents, you should create them through the Style dialog box and click in the Add to Template box. Then, when you create a document based on the template you added the styles to, the styles are available.

But even if you created styles with example paragraphs, you can get those styles into a new document by merging them. (This has nothing to do with the kind of merging that Chapter 15 dealt with; it simply means joining the styles from one place to another.)

Pull down the Format menu and choose Style. Click on the Define button and then, in the expanded Style dialog box, click on the Merge button. When the Merge Styles dialog box appears, change the text in the File Name text box from *.dot to *.**doc** because you want to merge the styles from a document, not a template. Then click OK.

Select the document you want to merge the styles from. Change directories if you need to in order to find the document. Word for Windows presents you with a dialog box telling you that Merging will replace the current styles with new styles of the same name. Do you want to replace the styles? Answer yes to this prompt and close the Style dialog box. Your new document now has the old document's styles available to you.

> **Doing the Template Merge Thing**
>
> Merging styles from one document to another can solve your immediate problem, but you still don't have those styles available when you create another new document, and you'll have to do the merge procedure all over again. If you anticipate needing those styles on a regular basis, use the same procedure to merge them to a template. Then, when you create a new document based on the template, you have the styles available. The only extra step you need to perform to merge the styles to a template is to click the To Template button in the Merge Style dialog box.

Problem 6:
You can't remember what's in your styles

A printed *style sheet* can be a useful reference when you need to know a style's attributes. To print a style sheet for your current document, even if it doesn't have text yet, pull down the File menu and choose **Print**. When the Print dialog box appears, choose Styles from the Print drop-down list. Click on OK and a list of styles and their attributes is sent to your printer.

Problem 7:
You can't remember how to change the style definition

If you want to change a style's attributes, just make the formatting changes to a paragraph with that style, click once on the name of the style in the style section of the ribbon, and then click back anywhere in the document. Word for Windows asks whether you want to redefine the style based on the selection. Answer yes, and all the paragraphs formatted with that style change to reflect the style's new attributes.

Problem 8:
After modifying the Normal style, other paragraphs look different

You have a document on the screen formatted with lots of terrific custom styles, and you decide that the paragraphs formatted with the Normal style should be double-spaced. So you follow the procedure described in the last problem. Oh no! Now *every* paragraph in your document is double-spaced. What the heck is happening here?

By default, when you create a new style it's based on whatever style is in effect for the current paragraph. This means that your new style includes any formatting you specify *plus* whatever formatting is included in the current style. This style is usually Normal because Normal is the default style. It makes sense, then, that if you change the attributes of the style another style is based on, *both* styles reflect the changes.

In the future, if you don't want certain styles to reflect changes you make to another style, don't base new styles on any existing styles. To create a new style that isn't based on any other style, pull down the Format menu and choose Style. Click on Define to expand the dialog box. In the expanded Style dialog box, select the name in the Based On box and press **Delete**.

For your current document, you can move to each paragraph you don't want double-spaced and specify single spacing from the Paragraph dialog box (accessed from the Format menu). You can also remove each of the other style's connections to a style by placing an insertion point in the paragraph you want to disconnect, pulling down the Format menu, choosing Style, and clicking on Define. Delete the name in the Based On box, click on the Change button, and then click on Apply.

Problem 9:
You can't figure out how to get out of a style

Every time you create a new paragraph it shares the style of the previous paragraph. If you don't like this feature, you can change it without having to pull down the Style list for every paragraph!

Word for Windows has a feature called Next Style, which lets you specify what the next style will be when the **Enter** key is pressed. To assign a Next Style, pull down the Format menu and choose Style. Select the style to which you want to add a Next Style from the Style Name drop-down list and

Take the Shortcut

Another easy way to apply and switch between styles is to assign shortcut keys to them. You may remember shortcut keys from the macros chapter; they work the same way for styles. When you create or modify a style in the opening Style dialog box, there is a Shortcut Key area with Ctrl and Shift already selected. Just choose a third key (usually a letter or a number) from the Key drop-down list and click on Apply. Now, whenever you want to use that style, just press the shortcut key combination.

click the Define button. Choose a next style in the Next Style drop-down list in the Change Formatting section. Click on Change and then click on Close. Pretty simple, eh?

Problem 10:

You can't use more than one line in a style that has a next style

Okay, you took my advice about that Next Style thing, and now you're mad at me because you can't type more than one line using the style that has a Next Style without switching to the next style.

The problem in this case isn't Word for Windows; it's the way you're typing. Instead of letting Word for Windows wrap words when it comes to the end of a line, you're inserting your own line breaks—which are really paragraph breaks, which drop you into the Next Style.

The solution is to *quit hitting Enter at the end of each line!* If you really need to break a line and you don't want to create a new paragraph, press **Shift+Enter**. This key combination inserts a new line without starting a new paragraph and keeps your styles intact!

Problem 11:

You can't remember which styles are applied to which paragraphs

The ribbon always displays the name of the style applied to the current paragraph. But if you want to see which style each paragraph is using, expand the *Style Area Width* by pulling down the Tools menu and choosing Options. In the Window area of the View category, increase the Style Width Area (usually about 0.5" will do it) to display each paragraph's style name down the left edge of the document.

> **Stylish Changes**
>
> If you have the Style Area Width expanded so you can see the style names, and you need to modify one of the styles, you can instantly get to the Style dialog box with that style selected by double-clicking on the style name to the left of the paragraph.

A Final Word on Styles

Styles can make your life with Word for Windows much easier. The reason some people don't use them is that they require a bit of planning. You have to decide *ahead of time* what styles to use and what attributes each new style will possess. As with many other aspects of your life, a little planning can pay off big-time.

Word for Windows Just Doesn't Work Right

CHAPTER NINETEEN

Now that you have all the major features of Word for Windows figured out and everything's running correctly, you should have smooth sailing from here, right? *Wrong!* You can trip over lots of little stumbling blocks on your way to the finish line. What you need are some stumbling-block busters.

Other Ways Word for Windows Can Leave You Speechless

Each of the preceding chapters in this section dealt with a specific problem area. But this chapter contains lots of little problems that just didn't fit in anyplace else. So if you haven't found your problem yet, this may be the chapter for you!

Fixing a Handful of Miscellaneous Problems

Are you having trouble hyphenating? Have you forgotten your password? Do you have your headers and footers upside down? If these problems sound familiar, take a peek at solutions that may just fit your problems.

Problem 1:
The "header" you typed at the top of each page is now in the middle of each page

After entering what you thought was a header at the top of each page, you enter some additional paragraphs to page one. The result, however, is that your "headers" ended up in the middle of each succeeding page. The cause for this problem is that you really didn't create a header, you merely typed text at the top of each page. When you inserted additional text, these fake headers moved in line with your other text.

The solution is simple—you need to learn how to use Word's header feature. Headers (or footers if you want your repeating text at the bottom of every page) let you type text that stays where it's supposed to, at the top of every page.

10 Do's and Don'ts That Didn't Fit Anyplace Else

1. *Do* use headers and footers for text you want repeated at the top or bottom of every page.

2. *Don't* use footnotes for repeating text; use a footer instead. A footnote is an annotation referring to a specific piece of text in the document.

3. *Do* use proportionally spaced fonts when you use justified alignment.

4. *Don't* use justified alignment without turning on automatic hyphenation or you'll end up with big ugly gaps between your words.

5. *Do* use manual hyphenation to break your words where *you* want instead of where Word thinks best.

6. *Don't* use Word's Annotation feature in place of footnotes. They usually don't print.

7. *Do* use Word's Outline view to organize groups of headings, subheadings, and paragraphs which you want to be able to promote or demote as a group.

8. *Don't* password-protect files. If you don't remember your password, the file is lost.

9. *Do* use Word's Draw feature to insert customized graphics into your document.

10. *Don't* create documents that are too long. Instead, create a *master document* and include all the smaller files you want to combine in it.

If your document has more than one section, the current section automatically inserts the previous section's header. If you change the header in the second section, the link to the previous section's header is broken. If you want to change the current header back to the header from the previous section, click on the Link to Previous button on the header bar. (If you haven't changed the header for the current section, the Link to Previous button is grayed out and unavailable.)

To create a header, you have to be in the Normal or Outline view; you can't create a header or footer from the Page Layout view. Pull down the View menu and select the Header/Footer option. Choose either Header or Footer, click OK, and you'll see the *header (or footer) creation window*. Type the text for your header or footer in this window. If you want to insert the page number, date, or time in the header, click on one of the buttons on the left side of the *header bar*. Click on the Close button and your header is created. It's only visible in Page Layout view or Print Preview or when you print the document.

Problem 2:
Justified text leaves big ugly gaps between some of the words

Yuck! I hate when that happens! This situation is most noticeable when you use fixed-width (monospaced) fonts. But even with proportional fonts, these gaps can occur. What's happening is that Word for Windows is adding space between words so the lines all have equal length. After all, that's essentially what you told Word for Windows to do when you specified justified alignment.

Some people think justified text looks more professional; I'm not one of those people. Besides, text without those gaps and with an uneven right margin (left-aligned) is often easier to read. I'd even go so far as to say that left-aligned text looks less pretentious.

As long as you insist on those even margins, there will be some gaps, but you can reduce the problem by turning on Word for Windows' Hyphenation feature. To hyphenate your document automatically, pull down the Tools menu, choose Hyphenation, and click on OK in the Hyphenation dialog box. Justified text also works better when you use a proportional-spaced font, which is just about anything but Courier or a built-in printer font. I've also found that the smaller your margins, the better justified text works. There aren't any perfect solutions to this problem, but following these tips should help things look better. If not, turn off the justification.

Problem 3:
Your footnotes don't print

This happens when you try to create footnotes with Word for Windows' Annotation feature. Annotations do work just like footnotes—except they aren't numbered and *they don't print*. Annotations are great for adding comments for the benefit of other people editing your document or giving yourself reminders. But if you want footnotes, use Word for Windows' Footnotes feature.

To create a footnote, position the insertion point next to the text you want to reference and pull down the Insert menu and select Footnote. Click on OK to accept Auto-Numbered Footnotes or click on the Custom Footnote Mark and enter the character you want to use for your footnote reference, such as an asterisk, and then click on OK.

Type whatever text you want to appear in your footnote at the bottom of the page and click on the Close button. If you create a footnote while in Page Layout view, there's no Close button, so just scroll back up to resume editing your document.

Problem 4:
You need to create an outline

Rather than just typing a bunch of text and separating headings from other text by pressing **Enter**, you'd like a way to keep headings of various levels organized. The solution is to create your document in

Word for Windows' Outline view. (Pull down the View menu and select the Outline option.) In Outline view, Word for Windows makes an outline out of your document automatically.

When you're in Outline view, you can promote headings to the next level up with **Alt+Shift+right arrow** or demote a headings with **Alt+Shift+left arrow**. Word for Windows applies standard heading styles to your various heading levels. You can modify the styles, and using heading styles makes creating a table of contents a snap. The great thing is, you can return to Normal or Page Layout view at any time, and you have a normal document!

Problem 5:
You can't open a password-protected file

You've created a very important, confidential document, so you password-protected it. Now you need to edit the file, but you forgot the password. This problem wouldn't be *so* bad, except that this is a *really* important file. Of course it is, or you wouldn't have password-protected it.

Unfortunately, there's no solution to this problem. Even Microsoft can't help you get your file back. If you password-protect a document, you'd better remember the password. If a file is that important and confidential, don't password protect it. Instead, just keep it on a diskette (backed up, of course) and lock the diskette in a safe place.

To password-protect a file, pull down the File menu, select the Save As option, and click on the File Sharing button. Type in a Protection Password. Word for Windows has you confirm it in the next dialog box. When you save the document, it's password-protected.

To open a file you've password protected, follow the normal procedures to open any normal file. Before Word for Windows opens the file, you're prompted to enter the password. Type the password EXACTLY the way you typed it when you assigned it to the file. If you're sure you typed the correct password but it didn't work, check the Caps Lock key. If the password was assigned in lowercase letters, that's how you need to enter it to open the file.

To remove password protection from a file, open the file (yes, you'll need to know the password to open it), pull down the File menu and select Save As. Choose File Sharing and then tap the **Delete** key to remove the password and choose OK. Click OK again to finish saving the file without the password. You can't remove password protection from a file if you've forgotten the password.

Problem 6:
You want to add a drawing to your document

When you're creating a document and you need to illustrate it with a drawing, you can create the drawing in Microsoft Draw, which is accessible through Word for Windows. Just pull down the Insert menu, select Object, and click on Microsoft Draw. The Microsoft Draw program appears, and you can create any sort of drawing you like.

When you close Draw, it asks whether you want to update the document. Answer yes to insert the drawing into the document. If you later need to modify the drawing, double-click on it and you'll be back in Draw with the drawing open.

> ### Draw on Que's Knowledge
>
> Microsoft Draw has quite a number of features in its own right, and you'll want to explore them all to take advantage of this powerful tool. Que's *Using Word for Windows 2,* Special Edition has information about how to use Microsoft Draw and the other useful applications that come with Word for Windows, which can't be covered in depth here.

Problem 7:
You're having trouble managing very long documents

When a file is too large, everything in Word for Windows slows down. Scrolling, spell checking, saving, opening—everything!

Because of this, you'd like to break documents into separate files of no more than about 50 pages each. The problem is that you want to be able to print all these shorter documents as one file with headers, footers, page numbers, and so on.

The solution to this problem is to create a *master document* to hook all the subdocuments together. To do this, insert *include* fields in a document, followed by the file names you want to include. Pull down the Insert menu, choose Field, and select Include from the Insert Field Type. Then type the file name in the text box following the include field and click on OK.

Repeat the procedure for each of the files you want to include in the master document. Now, when you print the master document, all these files are included. If you want to add a header or page numbering, add it to the master document, and it carries across to all the subdocuments.

Problem 8:
A hyphen you manually placed in a word at the end of a line remains visible when the word isn't at the end of a line

You press the hyphen (-) key to break a word in the correct place at the end of a line and everything seems just fine...until you add some text before the word and force the hyphenated word to the next line. Isn't Word for Windows smart enough to know that the hyphen should disappear if it's not needed? Yes it is! But only if you place the hyphen in the word in the correct way.

What you need to do is place an *optional* hyphen in the word by pressing **Ctrl+Hyphen** (-). If Word for Windows is displaying nonprinting characters, the optional hyphen displays as an L on its side. Don't worry, these optional hyphens won't print unless the word falls at the end of a line.

A Final Word on Getting Word for Windows To Work Right

I hope you found the solution to your problem in this chapter, but if you didn't, don't worry. I'm not through with you yet! The next section presents even more methods for getting yourself unstuck if you're still stuck. Word for Windows has so many features and ways to get to them that no one book (or even two or three) could possibly cover every situation. If you save your work regularly and then boldly experiment, you'll find the way to solve your own problem.

A Quick Course in Problem Solving

Word for Windows Error Messages— What They Mean and How To Deal with Them

Word for Windows uses error messages to try to tell you why something bad has happened. Some messages are easy to decipher, others are not. Because Word for Windows can display literally hundreds of error messages (some of them fairly obscure), I whittled down this chapter to the messages that you're most likely to encounter in Word for Windows.

I sorted the messages in alphabetical order and avoided including error messages specific to DOS or Windows—otherwise this book would expand by a few hundred pages. If your message isn't in this list, don't despair. Word for Windows' built-in help facility includes information about all the error messages you're likely to see. Check out the next chapter on getting help in Word for Windows.

A hyphenation error occurred. Word is ending the current session.

This error usually means that the hyphenation tool wasn't installed along with the rest of the Word for Windows program. Go through the installation process again and be sure to install all important files.

A spelling error occurred. Word is ending the current session.

This error means that Word for Windows is having a problem with its spell-checking program. Try reinstalling it from the original Word for Windows diskettes.

A thesaurus error occurred. Word is ending the current session.

This error usually means that the thesaurus wasn't installed along with the rest of the Word for Windows program. Go through the installation process again and be sure to install all important files.

Another window cannot be opened until one is closed

Word for Windows can only have nine document windows open at one time, and you've probably opened that many accidentally. Just close one or more of the open windows.

Application does not respond

You can get this message if you try to start another application, such as Microsoft Draw, from within Word for Windows and Word for Windows is low on memory. Try closing other running applications or adding more memory to your computer.

Bad file name

This message occurs if you create a macro that refers to a file that doesn't exist (or doesn't exist where the macro is trying to look for it). The solution is to change the macro so that it refers to an actual file name.

Copy from where?

When you press **Shift+F2** to copy text without first selecting the text you want to copy, Word for Windows gets confused. Go back and select the text you want to copy, and then press **Shift+F2** again.

`Do you want to change the properties of the standard style?`

When you modify one of the styles included with Word for Windows, you're prompted with this message so you can confirm that this is really your intention.

`Do you want to save the global glossary and command changes?`

Whenever you make changes which affect the NORMAL.DOT template, such as style, macro or glossary changes, you're prompted to confirm that you do indeed want to make these changes. You usually do.

`Document not open`

This message is another macro error. Your macro is referring to a document that is not open. Either change the macro or be sure the document is open when you run the macro.

`Error!`

This message indicates that you inserted a field with incorrect or insufficient instructions. The proper syntax for each field is displayed when you insert a field from the Field dialog box.

`Error! Cannot repaginate: no printer installed.`

Word for Windows repaginates documents based on the currently selected printer, so Word for Windows can't repaginate your document if no printer is installed or selected. Install a printer.

`Line spacing must be at least (measurement)`

You told Word for Windows to use line spacing less than your printer can handle. The (measurement) tells you what the smallest line spacing can be (usually 0.01 inch).

`Low memory. Close an application.`

If you run low on memory while you have other applications running in Windows, you may see this message. Close one or more of the other applications. In the future, either increase your computer's memory or run fewer applications.

`Low memory. Close extra windows and save your work.`

Take this one seriously! Save your work before you do anything else with your document. Then close any other open applications and see whether you can continue. If you can't, you may need to exit and restart Windows to free up enough system memory for your work at hand.

```
Low memory. Save the document now.
```
Do I need to explain this one? Save your document quickly! Close any other open documents or applications. If that doesn't solve the problem, you may need to add more memory to your computer.

```
Make a selection first.
```
If you try to move or copy text or graphics, but nothing is selected, this message appears on-screen. Select something and try again.

```
Move from where?
```
You pressed **F2** to move text without first selecting the text. Select the text you want to move and then press **F2** again.

```
Syntax error
```
You wrote a macro with an incorrectly structured command. But you don't write macros, you say? Well, this error can also happen if you edit a recorded macro and make a mistake. Word for Windows generally highlights the area of the macro that's causing the problem. If the flaw is obvious, fix it. Otherwise, call in a PC guru.

```
The disk is full
```
The destination disk or diskette is full, or you have too many documents open. Either clear some space from the disk by erasing some files, or close some documents.

```
The file is too large to save. Delete some text and
try again.
```
Not only do long documents slow you down—Word for Windows can actually choke on them. For this document, try cutting small chunks of text and pasting them to another document. In the future, use smaller documents and tie them together with a master document. Chapter 19 explains this concept.

```
The Next style name does not exist
```
If you try to add a Next style when creating or modifying a style, you must use a valid style name. If you get this message, try reentering the name for the Next style.

```
The password is incorrect. Word cannot open the
document.
```
Does the acronym SOL mean anything to you? In this case, it means that you're Simply Out of Luck, unless you have a version of this document not protected by a password. Remember those passwords! If you feel lucky, you might try retyping the password or checking Caps Lock and trying again.

```
The WINWORD.INI file is not valid. Word will use the
defaults.
```
If Word for Windows can't find the WINWORD.INI file or if the file is damaged, a new one is created and all the time you spent customizing defaults goes up in smoke! About all you can do at this point is to start customizing Word for Windows all over again or restore the WINWORD.INI to the WINWORD directory from your backup diskettes or tape.

```
There is a printer error
```
This message has a variety of causes, but the most common is low memory. Increase the available memory, perhaps by closing some documents or other applications, and try again.

```
There is not enough memory to...
```
Word for Windows displays various low-memory error messages, depending on what you're trying to do at the time. The specific message gives you a clue about what Word for Windows is having trouble with. Take the necessary steps to increase memory (close other applications or windows, delete unnecessary files) and try the action again.

```
This file is read-only
```
If you save a document as read-only or open a file as read-only so you can't accidentally alter it, you can't save it with any modifications. Either remove the read-only attribute or save the modified file under a different name.

```
Word cannot create a work file
```
Word for Windows needs space on a disk to create a work file for saving temporary editing changes. If the disk is full, you need to clear off some space. If you're on a network, this message may be

an indication that you are not properly connected to the network drive Word for Windows is looking for.

`You cannot base a style on itself`

If you try to create or modify a style and specify that it should be based on an existing style by the same name, you get this message. Base the style on another style, or don't base it on anything.

`You cannot change printer orientation with the current printer installed`

Some printers simply don't support landscape (horizontal) orientation. Your printer's documentation tells you whether the printer supports landscape. The solution for printers that don't print landscape is (don't laugh) to put the paper in sideways.

Getting Help in Word for Windows

CHAPTER TWENTY-ONE

Has this ever happened to you? You try to use a particular Word for Windows feature, such as changing margins, and you just can't remember where the darn feature is, or what it's called, or how to use it, or whether you even want to change margins after all.

Never fear! The purpose of this chapter is to show you how to get unstuck when you find yourself in a sticky situation. If you only read one chapter in this book, read this one!

How Word for Windows Helps You Get Unstuck

Do you ever find yourself staring at your computer screen, wondering what to do next? The next time this happens, turn to one of the many resources available to you.

Calling for Help

Of all the places you can turn for help while using Word for Windows, perhaps the fastest and most convenient is Word for Windows' built-in help system. You can find information about almost any aspect of Word for Windows without moving from your computer.

The easiest way to get help on a particular topic in Word for Windows is to pull down the Help menu and choose Help Index. Click on the Search button, and you can enter the name of any feature you're stuck on in the text box. As you start typing the feature's name, the list below the text box displays features starting with those letters.

When (perhaps I should say *if*) your feature appears in the list, click on it, and then click on the Show Topics button. A list of topics related to the selected feature appears in the topics list at the bottom of the dialog box. Select the topic you want and click on the Go To button. A help screen with information about your troublesome feature appears.

Getting Hyper

Many help screens have underlined words or phrases (usually in a lovely shade of green) to enable you to obtain additional information. If the word or phrase has a solid underline, it's called a *jump term*, and clicking on it displays a whole new help screen. If the text has a dashed underline, clicking on it displays a definition of the term.

You can close the definition box by clicking anywhere on the help screen. As you jump from one help screen to another, you can always move back to the previous screen by clicking on the Back button.

Jump terms and definition boxes are actually a form of *hypertext*, which is a technology that links related information in different parts of the help system. You can leap around from hypertext reference to hypertext reference all day long and never travel in a linear fashion. Hypertext help is all the rage these days because it makes it easier to find all the related information about unrelated topics.

> **Help Yellow Stickies**
>
> If there is a help screen you find yourself going back to repeatedly, consider marking it with a *Bookmark* so you can find it more easily next time. From the help screen you want to mark, pull down the Bookmark menu and choose Define. You can leave the topic name or enter something more meaningful to you and click on OK. The next time you want to go to that topic, choose Bookmark and click on the topic in the menu. If you want more than a placeholder, use the Annotate feature from the Edit menu. Type in any notes that will help you remember how to use the feature and then click on Save. A paper clip appears in the upper left corner of the help screen. Whenever you're at that help screen, you can look at your annotation by pulling down the Edit menu and choosing Annotate.

Putting Things in Context

You can instantly get a help screen for any highlighted item in a pull-down menu or any dialog box on-screen by pressing the Help key, **F1**. This kind of help is called *context-sensitive help* because it provides help that relates to what you're trying to do at the moment.

Pointing Out Some Help

Suppose you want some information about a portion of the Word for Windows screen. Or maybe you'd like to know how one of the keys on the keyboard works in Word for Windows. If you press **Shift+F1**, the mouse pointer turns into an arrow with a question mark attached. You can now point to any portion of the screen and click the left mouse button to display a help screen for that portion of the screen.

For example, press **Shift+F1**, move the tip of the arrow into the scroll bars, and click the left mouse button. Word for Windows shows you a scroll bar's help screen. If you want to find out what a key does, press **Shift+F1** and then press the key. For example, press **Shift+F1** and then press the **Shift+F2** to get a help screen on copying text.

Help for Word Perfectionists

If you're moving to Word for Windows from WordPerfect, those nice folks at Microsoft want to make your transition as easy as possible. To help you out, Word for Windows has special help for WordPerfect users. Pull down the Help menu and choose WordPerfect Help to display the Help for WordPerfect Users dialog box. Select a WordPerfect command from the Command Key list and then click on the Word Help button to see a help screen on how Word for Windows handles the feature.

With Demo selected in the Help Options section, you also can click OK to have Word for Windows demonstrate and execute the feature. As a final option, you can click on the Automatic Keys button so that you can use WordPerfect keys in Word for Windows. I don't recommend using the Automatic Keys feature because it just delays the Word for Windows learning process.

Who Ya Gonna Call?

If you think you've exhausted all the possibilities for getting yourself unstuck, you haven't. You can talk to a real live human being to get the information you need. No, don't call me; I'll be on a well-deserved vacation after writing this book. You may have a local PC guru who can get you going, but aren't these gurus always busy when you really need them?

When you need an answer, you need it now! Microsoft comes to the rescue with telephone technical support. You can call (206) 462-9673 between 6 A.M. and 6 P.M. (Pacific time) Monday through Friday. There is usually no more than a 10- or 15-minute wait before you are connected to a real live Word Wizard. The only charge for the service is the charge for the long-distance call.

A Final Word on Getting Help

There is no shame in getting stuck with your software. Just remember to use the help system, buy and read good reference books, and call Microsoft if you still need help. And don't forget to experiment with all of the

Using Your References

As wonderful as Word for Windows' help system is, you won't find all the answers in Help or even, I hate to admit, in this book. Many excellent Que books describe different facets of Word for Windows. And, as a reference, don't forget to take a look at the User's Guide included with Word for Windows.

wonderful features in Word for Windows. You'll probably learn more by experimenting than with any other method. Just a Word to the wise.

The Great Word for Windows Trouble-shooting Road Map

Here it is—the intrepid explorer's guide to working through all your Word for Windows problems! Just follow me and Mr. PC down the road until you come to the path that describes your particular problem. Read through the list of likely culprits for that problem, and then turn to the chapter noted. If you don't encounter any roadblocks, congratulations—Word for Windows is working just fine for you!

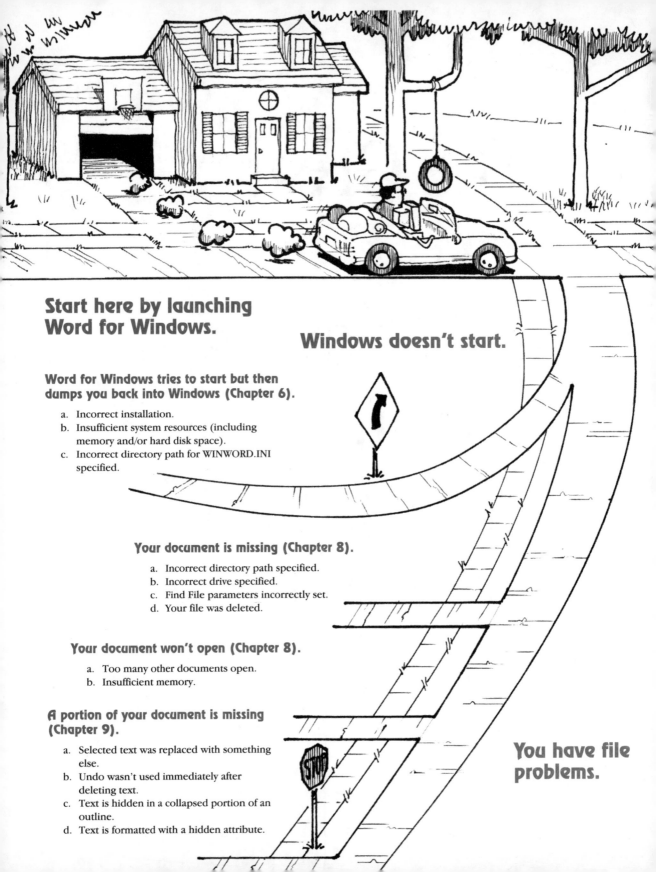

Start here by launching Word for Windows.

Windows doesn't start.

Word for Windows tries to start but then dumps you back into Windows (Chapter 6).

- a. Incorrect installation.
- b. Insufficient system resources (including memory and/or hard disk space).
- c. Incorrect directory path for WINWORD.INI specified.

Your document is missing (Chapter 8).

- a. Incorrect directory path specified.
- b. Incorrect drive specified.
- c. Find File parameters incorrectly set.
- d. Your file was deleted.

Your document won't open (Chapter 8).

- a. Too many other documents open.
- b. Insufficient memory.

A portion of your document is missing (Chapter 9).

- a. Selected text was replaced with something else.
- b. Undo wasn't used immediately after deleting text.
- c. Text is hidden in a collapsed portion of an outline.
- d. Text is formatted with a hidden attribute.

You have file problems.

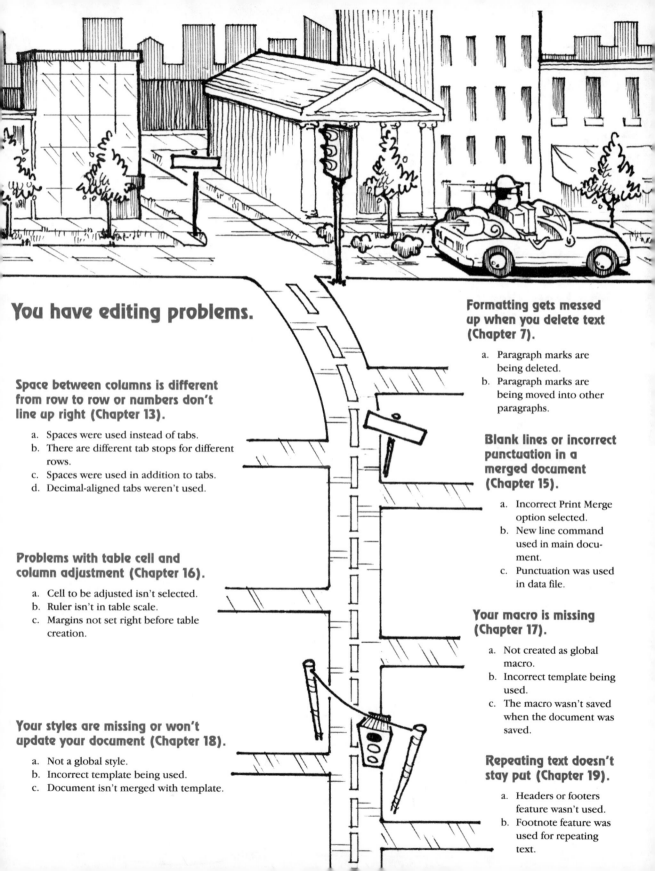

You have editing problems.

Space between columns is different from row to row or numbers don't line up right (Chapter 13).

a. Spaces were used instead of tabs.
b. There are different tab stops for different rows.
c. Spaces were used in addition to tabs.
d. Decimal-aligned tabs weren't used.

Problems with table cell and column adjustment (Chapter 16).

a. Cell to be adjusted isn't selected.
b. Ruler isn't in table scale.
c. Margins not set right before table creation.

Your styles are missing or won't update your document (Chapter 18).

a. Not a global style.
b. Incorrect template being used.
c. Document isn't merged with template.

Formatting gets messed up when you delete text (Chapter 7).

a. Paragraph marks are being deleted.
b. Paragraph marks are being moved into other paragraphs.

Blank lines or incorrect punctuation in a merged document (Chapter 15).

a. Incorrect Print Merge option selected.
b. New line command used in main document.
c. Punctuation was used in data file.

Your macro is missing (Chapter 17).

a. Not created as global macro.
b. Incorrect template being used.
c. The macro wasn't saved when the document was saved.

Repeating text doesn't stay put (Chapter 19).

a. Headers or footers feature wasn't used.
b. Footnote feature was used for repeating text.

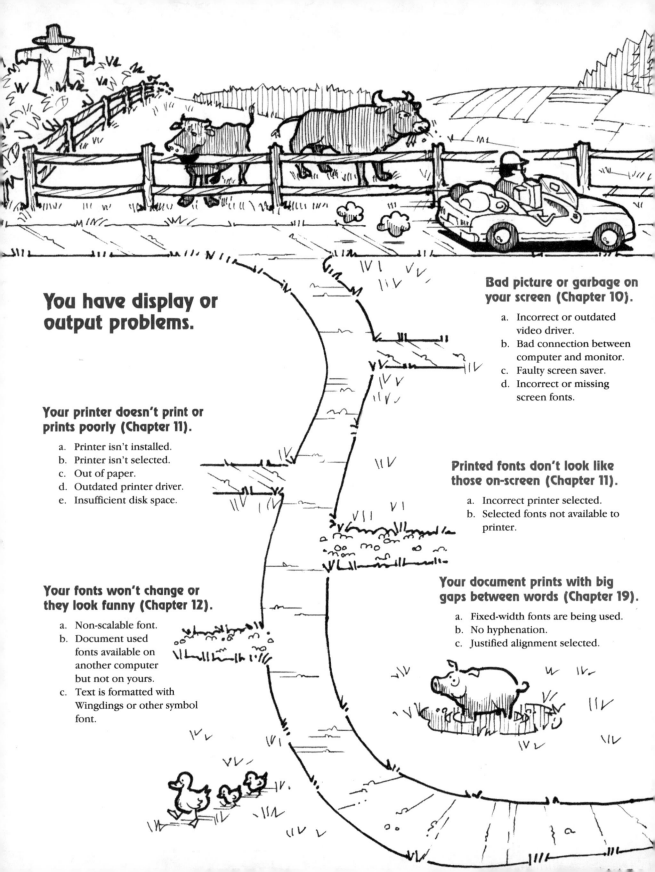

You have display or output problems.

Bad picture or garbage on your screen (Chapter 10).

a. Incorrect or outdated video driver.
b. Bad connection between computer and monitor.
c. Faulty screen saver.
d. Incorrect or missing screen fonts.

Your printer doesn't print or prints poorly (Chapter 11).

a. Printer isn't installed.
b. Printer isn't selected.
c. Out of paper.
d. Outdated printer driver.
e. Insufficient disk space.

Printed fonts don't look like those on-screen (Chapter 11).

a. Incorrect printer selected.
b. Selected fonts not available to printer.

Your fonts won't change or they look funny (Chapter 12).

a. Non-scalable font.
b. Document used fonts available on another computer but not on yours.
c. Text is formatted with Wingdings or other symbol font.

Your document prints with big gaps between words (Chapter 19).

a. Fixed-width fonts are being used.
b. No hyphenation.
c. Justified alignment selected.

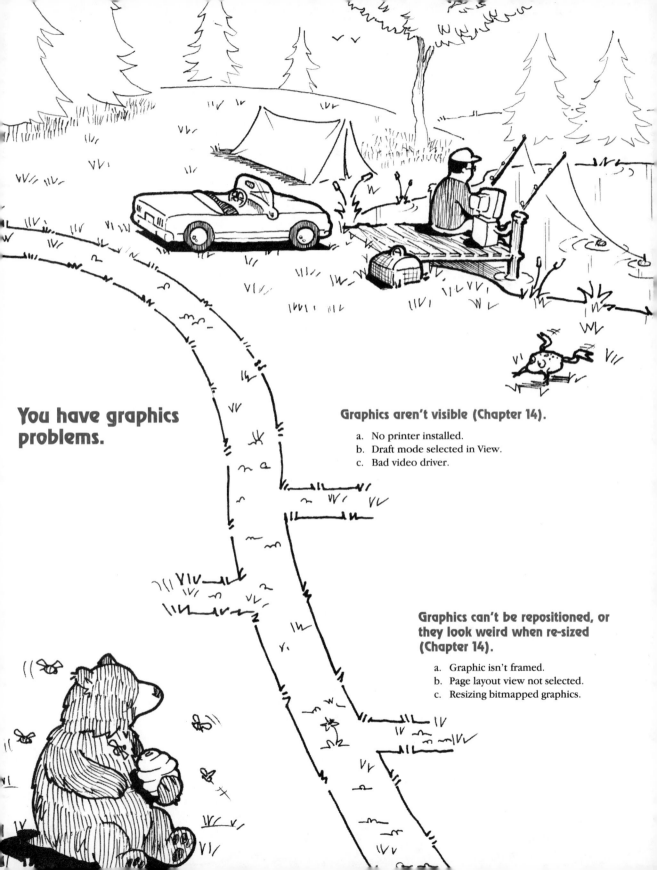

You have graphics problems.

Graphics aren't visible (Chapter 14).

a. No printer installed.
b. Draft mode selected in View.
c. Bad video driver.

Graphics can't be repositioned, or they look weird when re-sized (Chapter 14).

a. Graphic isn't framed.
b. Page layout view not selected.
c. Resizing bitmapped graphics.

The Oops! Word for Windows Glossary

application Another word for a computer software program.

back up The process of creating a copy of the data on your hard disk in case of an emergency.

bitmapped graphics Graphics made up of dots that correspond to the dots on-screen. Produced by painting programs.

bookmark A placeholder in Word for Windows that is used to locate or refer to parts of a document.

button An object in a window that can be "pressed" to perform specific operations by clicking on it with the mouse.

C: prompt The prompt issued by DOS when it is waiting

for you to enter a command. Also known as the *DOS prompt*.

click What you do with a mouse button. Usually pressing and releasing, as opposed to pressing and holding. (See *double-click*.)

Clipboard A special Windows memory area that stores the last cut or copied information. Clipboard data can be pasted to another location in the document or another application.

command Something you issue to start a task. In Windows and Word for Windows, certain menu options function as commands.

context-sensitive help On-screen assistance with the current task or command.

cursor The on-screen pointer.

data file A Word for Windows file containing the variable information to be combined with a main document during a print merge.

default The standard settings for a program. Word for

Windows uses defaults unless other options are chosen.

delete Erase. Kill. Zap. Get rid of.

dialog box An on-screen window that either displays a message or asks for user input.

directory A grouping of files on a disk; each directory can contain multiple files, as well as additional *subdirectories*.

diskette A portable disk. Also known as a *floppy disk*.

document window The window inside an application where your documents are created.

DOS The Disk Operating System for IBM compatible computers.

double-clicking Two quick clicks of the left mouse button.

drag and drop The action of using a mouse to move an object or selected text from one part of the screen to another.

dragging Moving the mouse while holding down the left mouse button.

error message   An on-screen message, usually displayed in a dialog box, generated by Word for Windows or Windows when something goes wrong.

fields   Codes that retrieve and display information from other sources, such as data files.

file   The data you store on your disks. All computer data is organized into files and all files have file names.

file name   The name assigned to a file. Each file name can contain up to eight characters followed by an optional period and an optional extension of up to three characters. DOC is the default extension in Word.

fixed-width fonts   A font in which every character occupies the same horizontal space on the line as every other.

font   In Word for Windows, font refers to the design of the typeface.

function key   One of the special keys labeled F1 through F10 or F12 on your computer keyboard.

global macro   A macro that is available in every document.

glossaries   Lists of graphics or text that can be retrieved by entering a shortcut name.

graphical user interface   A shell that uses pictures and objects to perform basic system tasks. Also known as a *GUI* (pronounced "gooey").

header   Text that repeats at the top of every page.

header row   The row containing the field names in a data file.

IBM-compatible   All personal computers that are compatible with the original IBM PC.

icon   A little picture that represents other objects or tasks, including software applications.

landscape   Print that is oriented sideways on the page.

macro   A series of commands or tasks that can be executed by issuing a shortcut name or key combination.

main document   The document containing the static information for a print merge.

master document   A document designed to facilitate the creation of a long document by including smaller sub-documents.

memory   Temporary storage for data and instructions, via electronic impulses on a chip.

menu bar   The area at the top of a window that contains a series of pull-down menus.

Microsoft   The company that publishes Windows and Word for Windows; disliked by competitors but loved by the stock market.

monitor   The screen that displays information from the computer.

multitasking   The ability to run more than one application at a time. (Windows works as a multitasking environment.)

Oops!   The sound you make when something goes wrong with Word for Windows.

operating environment   The pretty face that insulates you from the ugly interior of an operation system. (Windows is an operating environment.)

operating system   The core system software that communicates directly with your hardware. (MS-DOS is an operating system.)

overtype   The typing mode that replaces existing text as you type new text.

page layout view   Word for Windows' editing view that displays a close approximation of what the printed page will look like.

paragraph symbol   The symbol that represents the end of a paragraph (¶).

paste   To copy the contents of the Clipboard to a document.

path   The listing of the exact location of a file on a disk, including all directories and subdirectories.

pitch   The number of characters per inch in a fixed-width font.

pixel   The smallest possible portion of screen information. One dot.

point   A unit of measure, usually related to font size. One point is approximately 1/72 inch.

port   A fancy name for those connectors that stick out of the back of your system unit.

portrait   Print that is oriented normally (vertically) on the page.

print merge   An operation that joins information from a data file and a main document.

printer drivers   Small programs that translate instructions from an application to the printer.

Program Manager   The Windows program organizer and launcher.

proportional fonts   Fonts in which each character occupies the appropriate horizontal space (rather than a standard space).

RAM   Random-Access Memory. A type of temporary, working memory used by your computer to contain what you're working on right now. Everything contained in RAM ceases to exist when your computer is turned off, yet another reason to save often.

record   A group of related fields (one row) in a data file.

resolution   The amount of screen detail of a screen image.

ribbon   The Word for Windows graphical bar used for viewing and applying character formatting.

ruler   A visual position reference that can be used for certain paragraph, table, and column formatting.

sans serif fonts   Typefaces that don't have decorations on their ends.

scroll bars   The bars at the side and bottom of a window that enable you to scroll through the complete window area.

select   Highlighting by dragging the mouse over text or clicking on an object.

selection bar A blank vertical strip on the left side of the document used for selecting large portions of the document.

serif fonts Typefaces with decorations on their ends.

status bar Displays information about position and status of your current document. Located at the bottom of the document.

style A group of formatting instructions that can be applied to a paragraph.

style sheet The group of styles available in a particular document.

subdirectory A subsidiary directory located off a main directory.

system unit The part of your computer system that looks like a big beige box and contains lots of important electronic parts.

tab stop A relative distance from the left margin, reached by pressing Tab an appropriate number of times.

table A grid of rows and columns for organizing text and numbers.

tabular tables Rows and columns separated by tabs and paragraph marks.

template A collection of formatting settings which provide a basis for Word for Windows documents.

title bar The bar at the top of a window which displays the application's or document's title.

toolbar The graphical bar that provides icon buttons that are shortcuts to commonly used tasks.

vector graphics Graphics made up of discrete objects, such as those produced in drawing programs.

VGA Video Graphics Array. A Windows display standard.

window An on-screen space surrounded by a frame and containing either a complete application or a document.

Windows A multitasking operating environment from Microsoft that runs on top of DOS and provides a graphical user interface.

word wrap Word for Windows' ability to break lines when words extend beyond the right margin, eliminating the need to press **Enter** to end lines.

WYSIWYG What-You-See-Is What-You-Get, which means that what you see on-screen is (sort of) what you'll get out of your printer.

Index

F

H

header row, 269
Header/Footer command (View menu), 238
headers, 15, 236-238, 269
Help, 10-11, 256
    context-sensitive, 257, 268
    hypertext, 257
    jump terms, 256
    technical support, 258
    topics, 256
Help Index command (Help menu), 10, 256
hidden text, 108-109, 112-114, 128
highlighted format, 104
hypertext, 257
hyphenation, 238, 242, 248
Hyphenation command (Tools menu), 238

I

icons, 22, 269
    Color, 128
    Fonts, 126, 136
    Printers, 134
    Program, 75-76
    properties, 71
    Word, 43
importing
    files, 102-103
    graphics, 183-184
    import filter, 184
include fields, 242
insert mode, 85
Insert Rows command (Table menu), 207

inserting
    graphics, 177-178, 181
    rows (tables), 207
    tables in documents, 208
    text, 81-85
insertion point
    deleting text, 108
    inserting text, 81
    moving, 81
    positioning, 85
    tables, 203
installation, 66
    dialog boxes, 66
    fonts, 127
    printers, 134
    Setup program, 66
interlaced display, 125

J–K

jump terms (Help), 256
justification, 238-239
keyboard
    assigning keys to macros, 217
    Backspace key, 82
    Caps Lock key, 12
    Delete key, 82
    F1 (Help), 10
    function keys, 269
    scrolling, 80-81
    selecting text, 83

L

landscape orientation, 32, 269
laser printers, graphics, 185
launching, see starting
left tab, 165

updating graphics, 184
uppercase text, 12
Use as Default button (Character dialog box), 156

V

variables (merges), 190
vector graphics, 272
vertical-refresh rate, 126
video cards, 118
video display driver, 118
video drivers, graphics, 181
viewing
 columns, 129
 fonts, 126
 graphics, 180
 text, 111-112
views
 Draft, 88, 119
 Normal, 119
 Page Layout, 15, 120, 270
 Print Preview, 15

W

warm boot, 59
Windows, 22-23, 272
 File Manager, *see* File
 Manager
 printing, freezes, 141
 Program Manager, *see*
 Program Manager
 restarting, 60

windows, 23, 28-29, 272
 document window, 268
 header/footer creation, 238
 opening multiple, 248
 scrolling, 80
Wingdings, 159
WINWORD directory, 71
Word
 data file backups, 54
 icon, 43
 original disks, 53-54
 starting
  double clicking file name, 72-73
  from File Manager, 68, 71-72
  from Program icon, 67, 71
  from Run command, 68, 72
word processing, 24-25
word wrap, 14, 25, 203, 273
working directory, 12
WYSIWYG (What-You-See-Is-What-You-Get), 44, 118-119

X–Y–Z

Zoom command (View menu), 110